Pro-te-us (pro te œs), n. **1.** *Class.* Myth. A sea god, son of Oceanus and Tethys, noted for his ability to assume different forms and to prophesy. **2.** A person or thing that readily changes appearance....

PROTEUS
Insights from 2020

Compiled by Pamela H. Krause

Written by Michael S. Loescher,
Chris Schroeder, and
Charles W. Thomas

As individuals, our futures are certain. Because it is, the art of enlightened living lies in the moment. Four thousand years of collective philosophy across the cultural panoply of human civilization echoes the same thought. Death – the certainty of tomorrow – bounds, shapes, encapsulates, defines the human experience. *Tempis fugit.*

Not so with our enterprises – a nation, a tribe, a company, a cult – we build and leave behind. Our enterprises are the collective efforts of generations, the repositories of what we know and all that we safeguard. For an enterprise, the future is an uncertain place. Risk is certain, and it must be managed. This is especially so for an intelligence organization, charged as we are with managing uncertainty for national security.

For a decade, we have all struggled to understand the post-Cold War period. We have not even known what to call it without borrowing from the past: the "post-Cold War." Meanwhile, the turbulence and complexity of the world has been building and swirling about us day by day, played out in succinct sound bytes on the nightly news. By now, we have seen enough, surely, to understand that the rubble of the Berlin Wall is being used not to model the past, but to build a genuinely New Age. The underpinnings of world order have shifted fundamentally, and the very natures of wealth, power, sanctuary – and national security – are shifting beneath our feet.

The question for us, I think, is not how the future will unfold – we cannot predict that with clarity. We must wait until we get there to see how it turns out. The questions are, rather, how we can face the future, react to it, operate in it, and understand it. It is our posture that matters. For that, we must find new approaches to planning that affords us deeper looks at the shifting bedrock and not leave us reacting to the aftershocks.

This document is unique in my experience in Government. It is neither an analysis, nor a plan for the future. Nor is it a guess at how the future will be. Rather, it is an unusually rich and thoughtful collection of insights about the problems of 2020. Specifically, it is about the problems that the U.S. Intelligence Community might face and how we might see the future through something other than the distorted lens of the present.

The *Proteus* Insights are the result of nearly 18 months of effort involving some of the best minds in the country – from poets to intelligence professionals – brought together by the National Reconnaissance Office to examine how we might come to grips with the future. For me, there were some major surprises in the findings, and I have directed the team to continue its work. I urge you to read on. Take notes in the margins. Dog-ear the pages. Study. Nothing is what it seems; the future all the more so.

David A. Kier
Deputy Director
National Reconnaissance Office
November 2000

T his book is a testament to teamwork and the desire to ensure a strong national future. Literally hundreds of people have given their time and lent their professional talents to the development of these Insights.

Chief among them is Charles W. Thomas of Deloitte Consulting, who is perhaps the nation's leading futurist and the inventor of the scenario-based planning technique we used. Armed with a brilliant process, great experience, and even greater patience, it was he who led us into the future that you see in these pages.

All of the words and many of the ideas in the book are those of Michael S. Loescher of the Copernicus Institute. For more than 15 years he has been one of the leading and most prolific commentators on future warfare and intelligence matters. He has a gift for clarity at the white board and the keyboard, for which we are grateful.

To Project Manager Chris Schroeder, Tom Simpson of Litton-TASC, and Tom Witherell of Veridian-PSR we owe much for their diligence, skills in organization and management, and remarkable prescience into the present and future of intelligence. Without them, we would have wandered off into the wild blue.

Our core team – many of whom stayed with us for more than 18 months despite heavy commitments in their own jobs – chose the drivers and dimensions and built the characteristics matrix for the five *Proteus* worlds. Among them were: Dennis Andrucyk, Jay Berman, Don Call, Rob Callum, Martha Culver, Bob Flynn, Nancy Forbes, Dave Gessert, Mike Hall, Steve Hotaling, Pete Kennedy, Rob Klotz, Ben Lamb, Bob Lanahan, Bruce Martin, Steve Meade,

Lindy Moran, Rob Odell, Julie Turner, Bud Uyeda, Jeff Vance, Kim Walls, and H.R. Zucker.

To gain our Insights, we held three workshops. In May 1999, our participants were: Tron Alexander, Margaret Barnstead, Rena Batts, Jack Bowden, Ken Bradley, Larry Burgess, Angela Burns, Jerry Cameron, Robert Chambers, Chris Chapin, Kelsey Christopher, John Conover, Tom Conroy, Mary Corrado, Tommy Crawford, Joseph Culver, David Czzowitz, Tom Darner, Mary Delap-Snyder, Bob Dickman, Sue Duclos, Keith Dugger, Rand Fisher, Dennis Fitzgerald, Rose Flanery, Janet Gale, Tom Garin, Carolyn Gavares, Chuck Gibson, Jeff Graham, Will Gregory, Bong Gumahad, Bob Haase, Pat Hanback, Gary Harmon, Karen Hinkle, Kawana Hutson, Karl Jensen, Rob Johnson, Fred Kennedy, Gil Klinger, Denise Knox, Julia Kortum, Julie Laderach, Rich Lajoie, Ray Longerbeam, Bob McCants, Richard McCormick, Thomas Malarkey, Barbara Male, Bill Manzanares, Raley Marek, Roger Marsh, Scott Meisinger, John Miller, Kevin Missar, Page Moffett, Rob Myhre, Jim Norman, Rick Oborn, Sparkey Olsen, Ed Patneaud, Tanya Pemberton, Kelly Pickering, Rod Potter, Tom Quigley, Mike Reese, Joseph Reft, Ken Renshaw, Pam Richards, Sean Roche, Mike Rosas, Betty Sapp, Jon Sastri, Susan Shekmar, Joseph Sovey, Frank Strickland, Renee Strickland, Garnett Stowe, Bob Surrette, Dave Svetz, Tom Tillotson, Dave Tolliver, Steve Tomanelli, Mike Toth, Jennifer Walsmith, Pat Warfle, Dan Wells, Doug Westphal, Steve Wojcicki, and Doug Wolfe.

In September 1999, we brought together a remarkable, eclectic group, most of whom were outsiders to the Intelligence Community: Eric Anderson, Lori Austin, Robert Avila, Fred Beaudry, Robert Blair, Kent Bond, Paul Bracken, Sheila Buckley, Janet Burnham, Tony Burshnick, Anne Cahn, John Casti, Jack Clarke, Danny Cohen, John Cramer, Thomas Crumm, Chris Elvidge, Robert Forward, Hank Gaffney, Alan Gaines, Patricia Garfinkel, T.J. Gilmartin, Norman Graham, Christopher (Kit) Green, Joe Greenblott, Ted Hagelin, Denny Harman, David Hartley, Malina Hills, Howard Hirano, Chris Holmes, Neil

Jacobstein, Jamie Jisa, Peter Jutro, Tom Knight, Rob Kutz, Dan LaLiberte, Lee Lunsford, Bob Manoff, Ralph Merkle, Kevin Miller, Stephen Morse, Tommy Murphy, John Parmentola, George Patrick, Robert Pearce, John Peterson, Joe Pilat, Thomas Prudhomme, Alan Shaw, Brian Shaw, Irvin Stiglitz, Joyce Tichler, Haydn Wadley, Kenneth Walker, Fred Wergeles, Scott Wetterhall, Ray Williamson, and lastly, Kristin Zimmerman.

In October 1999, we experienced our five worlds with some of the most experienced intelligence professionals in the country: George Adaniya, Phil Anselmo, Keith Barber, Grace Bassler, Ivan Bekey, Larry Birckelbaw, Brad Bogan, Patrice Cassine, Steve Clark, Phil Curran, Greg Davis, Jim Devine, Al DiMarcantonio, Nick Eftimiades, Dave Frediani, Ron Goldberg, Dan Goure, Rob Hargis, Rich Haver, Darrell Herd, Lillie Hill-Martin, Malina Hills, Chandler Hirsch, Jerry Hirsch, Jim Holden, Robin Holliday, Terry Howell, Peter Jutro, Ray Koym, Frank Mahncke, Ted Mandro, Art Manfredi, Joe Markowitz, Bob Martinez, Marty McCabe, Glen McWright, Kristin Meegan, Pete Merkle, Bob Minehart, Julian Nall, Rich Nibe, Mal O'Neill, Paul Pattak, Tom Reglein, Greg Rhoney, Aaron Robertson, Ron Russell, Chris Schneider, Al Schuler, Erica Sciance, George Sims, Jim Skoulikas, Rob Stearns, Cindy Stellman, Ivan "Doc" Taylor, Lee Tilton, Annette Totten, Eric Viglione, Tammy Villaneuva, John Wangsgard, Dick Winslow, Steve Witek, Andy Wright, Gerry Yonas, and finally, Barbara Yoon.

Finally, special thanks to the NRO leadership for providing the freedom and inspiration to pursue this Study.

Pamela H. Krause
Project Director
National Reconnaissance Office
November 2000

TABLE OF CONTENTS

S ince the beginnings of human existence, explaining the past and predicting the future have preoccupied us. As in every age since the Greek Herodotus wrote his first *Histories*, his successors today are revising our view of what happened in the lives of those before us. Revisionist history is not just a recent phenomenon; we have all tried, one generation after another, to come to understand the past in order to make sense of the present in which we live. Already, hundreds of books have been published on the Cold War, only a decade after the collapse of the Soviet Union. Time yields perspective.

We all want human existence to have a sense to it. The role of historians – mostly professional academics, until recently – has been to find that sense by placing the past into some apparent logical construct. Looking backward, we can construct patterns as we wish.

It is harder for predictors of the future. In the skeptical, secular world of today, the prevailing view has become that the future cannot be foreseen. If science cannot do it, then it cannot be done. Yet, it is a difficult urge to deny – fortune-tellers, seers, and not a few pundits still make a living at it, from villages to Wall Street. And, more to the point of this research effort, thousands of "strategic plans" and "master plans" are on the shelves of the world's enterprises today with more being added daily. Most reflect the human propensity to extrapolate the present and the past into the future – nothing is new under the sun.

In recent years, however, this approach has led to some stunning failures. The rise of the New Economy, with its fundamentally new value chain, certainly could not have been predicted by classical economic planning. The implosion of the Soviet Union was another. When we look at the future through the lens of past experiences and with the arrogance that the future is knowable, we set ourselves up not only for change, but also for surprise. No master plan extrapolated from the present of 1970 could have predicted the rise of the Internet or the Falun Gong in the 1990s.

In the past 150 of the 100,000 years or so that *Homo sapiens* has been knocking about the planet, we have been exposed to some truly earth-shaking realizations. Darwin told us we descended from apes. Shortly thereafter, we evidently ate the Neanderthals. The very ground on which we stand is moving at about one inch per year; its edges either diving into the center of the planet or rising up into mountain peaks. Einstein told us time did not exist. NASA has found hundreds of planets out there. Sequences of four amino acids define genetic makeup. It turns out there are black holes, worms in space, and billions of tons of invisible antimatter. Sheeesh – what next?

§

Indeed. This book is the first product from the *Proteus* Project, sponsored by the National Reconnaissance Office (NRO) to investigate new methodologies and technologies for intelligence collection and analysis. Born out of the space race and the Cold War, the NRO has been the nation's core repository of intellectual capital and high technology for intelligence systems for 40 years. *Proteus* is one of a number of parallel efforts underway within the NRO to examine its future roles in safeguarding national security and to devise new systems and processes necessitated by an increasingly complex world.

The *Proteus* study itself consists of four efforts. This book details the findings of the first effort, an exploration of potential problems for the Intelligence Community in 2020. In it, we offer no solutions or strategies. They come later, and our approach to the remaining efforts is described in Chapter 11. In the pages that follow – as in the real future, no doubt – there is good news, bad news, and uncertain news. There are some bewildering conclusions and some genuinely frightening developments. We describe these findings in the next chapters. Each of these *Insights* contains genuinely new observations about the future, and we have attempted to explore their implications for the Intelligence Community. Our nine *Insights* are:

- *Starlight*: the role and nature of time in analysis
- *Sanctuary*: the propensity to hide in a open world
- *Small Stuff*: software, biotechnology, and nanotechnology
- *Veracity*: the challenge of truth and knowledge
- *Herds*: people and ideas on the move
- *Wealth*: moving past money
- *Power*: clout and who or what has it
- *A Parallel Universe*: from networks to cyber life
- *Bedfellows*: the significance of teaming

Strange titles to convey *Insights* of 2020 to the largely technical audience of intelligence professionals for whom this book is written! We have a purpose in doing so. Human beings learn in one of two ways, either by categorization or by metaphor. In our busy scientific and technologically oriented world, we tend to defer to the first. In other words, we look for patterns we recognize. The problem with that logic is, of course, that we overlook those patterns that we do not recognize right away.

This propensity to leap to conclusion is not just a peccadillo of the Intelligence Community. In the modern world, where logic has trumped intuition for many of us, it is increasingly prevalent. In part, it is what we have learned in our schooling: deduction and logic can be measured (and graded on the bell curve), but intuition and nuance are much harder to understand. Without doubt, the urge for logic, frameworks, charts, graphs, equations, and measures of effectiveness have taken us far. But the search for precision has its dangers as well. In this book, we are concerned with three in particular.

First, there is a tendency to categorize what is not quantifiable as either irrelevant or incomplete. Yet, there are things that cannot be quantified: fear, hate, and loyalty among them – all-powerful forces in our world.

Second, logic is, at its core, a reductionist framework. It seeks precision in relationships by directly relating one phenomenon to another. But reductionism is both impatient and hardheaded. Reductionism drives us to make fast conclusions based on what we have seen before – it is essentially the process of compartmentalizing what we observe. By doing this, we tend to make the packets fit preconceived ideas, however much we have to jam them in place. The net result is that we construct futures that are self-realizing. When it becomes the habitual way in which we think, we leave ourselves open for surprise.

Finally, deduction limits learning — it is a bit like reducing music to a collection of simultaneous frequencies. True enough, but much is missed. As every parent knows, children begin with intuition and find patterns in ways we no longer can. At first, all green things outside the window grow together. Some then become trees; others bushes. Later in life, when frameworks are passed on, the green things become genera and species. By then, unless we remain intellectually youthful, the big green thing in the yard is forever a maple, a label lost on the tree.

Metaphor, in the grand sense of the word (yes, Miss Smith, we know the difference among similes, metaphors, analogies, and parables), gives us much, especially when used as a companion to logic. Metaphor often is the source of first innovation. Edison said the idea for the light bulb came to him in the analogy of better oil lamps. Almost all of what we know the world over about religion is metaphor. Consider three of the most beautiful and what they add to our understanding. First, from the Koran:

> God has made a polish for everything that tarnishes.
> And the polish for the heart is remembrance.

And, the pastoral simplicity of Psalm 23:

> The Lord is my shepherd; I shall not want.
> He maketh me to lie down in green pastures:
> He leadeth me beside still waters.

Finally, from the Tao Te Ching:

> The great Tao floods and flows in
> every direction.
> Everything in existence depends on it,
> and it doesn't deny them.

Thus, what we offer here is a set of metaphors that describe the notional problem space for the future Intelligence Community. A couple of examples illustrate what we have found, and we hope spurs you on to the remaining chapters.

- We believe the merger of sophisticated software, biotechnology, and nanotechnology will change our very definition of what life *is*, with the disturbing implication that new and very powerful "life" forms may emerge to upset our understanding of power and wealth in the world.

- The completion of the global Internet infrastructure early in the 21st century sets the stage for a massive uploading of knowledge serviced by very sophisticated computing technologies. We believe this phenomenon can be best understood by thinking of it as a digital "Cambrian Explosion" in which silicon life takes on a form of evolution analogous to, but not the same as, biological natural selection. Understanding the mechanics of this kind of evolution and the digital ecology that arises to foster it may be a key intelligence problem in the future.

- Similarly, we believe that trying to define and understand Information Operations (and its attendant Information Warfare doctrine) in terms of network topology is a dangerously limiting concept. Despite the enormous sum that has been spent in that direction, we suggest that trying to understand IO/IW through detailed network topology and data tags is like trying to understand life in Manhattan by studying the geology of the island.

- We have found evidence of a frightening possibility that a fundamentally new kind of knowledge may be emerging – a kind of mutable knowledge that can be isolated from truth or falsehood and left to exist in the absence of either. Neither intrinsically true nor false, the new form of emerging knowledge could become extremely powerful in a wired world.

- It appears, counter-intuitively, that the more open the world becomes, the more closed it becomes at the same time. In the future, pursuit of sanctuary is big business. In the future we all can run, and we all can hide.

- Everywhere we went in the future, the temporal world took on increasing importance over the physical world. In the future it turns out time is not only money; it is the principal component of power, ideas, organizations, events, intent, and veracity.

§

Each of our *Insights* was gained through the work of many participants. Our work was accomplished employing a proprietary Deloitte Consulting/Futures Group scenario-based planning methodology, which is explained in more detail in Appendix A. It is enough here to say that we developed five plausible future worlds of 2020. Each was specifically designed and written to present the Intelligence Community multiple challenges within the context of complex political, sociological, and economic settings. In other words, the scenarios were not war games designed to explore specific problems – another aspect of the Study is intended to do that. Rather, the worlds were built in such a way that the participants were forced to use their individual and collective professional experience to find the intelligence challenges.

It is useful for the reader to understand the essential elements of each of our five worlds before turning the pages to the *Insights* that follow. The worlds are summarized below, and the full narratives are presented in Appendices B-F.

Amazon.plague is a world wracked by highly contagious, deadly viruses that flare up, die down, and then return in mutated form. Efforts to contain and counteract the plagues have been only marginally effective. Consequently, trade and commerce have dried up and the world's economy has declined sharply. The globe is now mired in a serious, long-term recession. Nations have tended to either become authoritarian or succumb to chaos. The U.S. and a few other resilient countries with relatively low fatality rates have signed a mutual assistance treaty to find the cure and protect each other's security interests. These "viable" states have sealed their borders to shield themselves from constant mass migration attempts from less fortunate neighbors.

In the U.S., the Democratic and Republican parties have given way to "Greens" and "Techs". Greens seek a return to basic living and tend to blame technology for the world's evils, while the Techs look to medical research and technology to solve the plague crisis. Power increasingly resides in community groups and local health centers, most of which are connected to and supported by the federal government. The public has generally agreed to sacrifice some personal freedoms in favor of medical IDs and increased surveillance of potentially "unhealthy" populations. The Internet has evolved into the Global Information Grid, which has become the preferred method of commerce, communication, and education in this disease-ridden world.

The Enemy Within is a world in which the U.S. has slowly, unexpectedly, and quite dramatically unraveled. Like so many other nations at the height of power, our disagreements, ethnic tensions, and single-issue politics have torn the social fabric. Our society is fractured and fragmented – politically, socially, and culturally. Intergenerational strife, compounded by record unemployment, has torn apart our churches, neighborhoods, and families. Racial tensions are a tinderbox in cities, suburbs, and rural America.

In this uncivil society, the specter of imminent collapse looms over everyday activity. Violence can pop up at any time and in the most unlikely places. There seems to be no refuge. Under such social circumstances, capital and business are flowing out of the country. The nation's economy creaks along at barely sustainable levels. Agriculture, health care and pharmaceuticals, low-end retail, personal security services, and construction are among the few bright spots in this abysmal economy. Government coalitions struggle to find an appropriate national response to the seemingly never-ending crisis. All other national tasks and obligations take a back seat as the country turns inward to face the most critical turning point of its 250-year history.

Militant Shangri-la is a world of unexpected events and difficult-to-trace villains. The world in general, and the U.S. in particular, has continued into a third decade of a prosperous, information-driven economy. But the world is also continuing along the road to complexity, with new structures of influence throughout the globe. The Newtonian diplomatic and military calculus of the past 400 years, since nation-states emerged at the end of the Middle Ages, seems to be giving way to a new Age. In particular, the global man-in-the-street has endured the past century of 200 million deaths in war, endured dizzying and difficult technological change, and is listening sympathetically to the Earth groan under the burden of pollution and extinction. Nearly all of the animals of Africa, many of the fish in the sea, and much of the wild areas of the globe are used up.

Into this world enters the new and worrisome Alliance of the Southern Constellation: South Africa, India, Indonesia, China, and other pariahs to the Western social philosophy of individual liberty and human rights, operating both legitimately as a block of aligned nation states and illegitimately as criminal cartels. Their grand strategy is to keep the world on the edge of chaos, and from that chaos, reap profit. The Alliance is in space, on the seas, in the media and financial institutions, and worming into the hearts and minds of individuals, killing the very idea of personal liberty. Meanwhile, the U.S., its four English-speaking cousins, Japan, and a newly unified Korea have united to resist this evil empire.

New Camelot is a world in which times are good for the U.S. and most of the world. We enjoy economic growth, international stability, technological progress, and the fruits of an energy breakthrough that promises cheap fuel and a clean environment. Most American citizens sleep soundly without worries of global conflicts, physical threats, or financial insecurities. Large, horizontally integrated, global corporations drive strong consumer markets and keep products, services, ideas, and technology flowing across all borders. The global economy churns with machine-like efficiency.

The U.S. no longer dominates militarily and economically, but at a time of rising affluence and an ever-improving quality of life, nobody cares. The U.S. government is still very involved and assertive in world affairs. For the first time in anyone's memory, the past is not looked back on wistfully as the "good old days." A confluence of factors got us here – globalization, governmental reform, and information, among them – and they promise to sustain forward progress. There are, of course, no guarantees. Not all the world is sharing equally in these good times. Some nations are left out, perhaps too far behind in skills and infrastructure to play in this very competitive, free, and global marketplace. But the mood is bright, government is visionary, firms are dynamic, and we all believe in the future.

Yankee Going Home is a world in which little is clear except that the world has changed in fundamental ways. Who is running things? Why are certain decisions made? What goals are being pursued? Who are friends and who are enemies? The U.S. has withdrawn from the world, gone home after a series of terrible foreign policy blunders and after a longstanding and deep recession. The world is heavily influenced by the memories of terrorism, regional war, and worldwide instability that followed the U.S. retreat.

The world that emerges is made up of both traditional actors (nations, international organizations, non-government organizations) and powerful non-traditional actors (global corporate alliances, criminal groups, mercenary units). These actors cooperate for power and influence while simultaneously competing for position and control in a constant whirl of politics and economics, bewildering to nearly all concerned. In this world, historical notions of allegiances are questioned, and the rules of the game are difficult to understand. Predictable behavior becomes the unique exception rather than the expected standard.

§

Before describing our insights into the future, we think it is useful to share a preliminary insight we gained into the present. Chiseled into the stone above the entrance of the ancient Temple of Apollo in Delphi was the famous admonition "Know Thyself." By this phrase, finally, the *Proteus* core team came to understand one of our most interesting findings – about the nature of the intelligence professionals that took part in this effort.

In the course of the Deloitte Adopt-a-World™ workshops, the intelligence professionals were divided among the five worlds and forced to operate strictly within the constructs and constraints of the scenarios and to find a consensus in a relatively short time. For some, the experience intellectually was stimulating. For others, it was frustrating. In the end, however, an identifiable set of patterns began to appear in watching the groups work collectively to develop their recommended courses of action to the problems presented by their worlds.

As a group, the participants had a strong propensity to find – or even create – traditional threats. In doing this, they tended to miss or misconstrue the non-traditional threats. This, in itself, is perhaps not too surprising for a group of highly technical, largely middle-aged, post-Cold Warriors. The surprise came in the clarity of the cases, which gave us some broad insight into the *group nature* of blindness in intelligence organizations:

- When the *problem* – the background forces for change – was clear and the *threat* was clear, the groups were comfortable and moved only slightly out of the box in finding solutions.

- When the *problem* was clear, but the *threat* was ambiguous, the groups were uncomfortable, but engaged in innovative thinking.

- When the *problem* and the *threat* were ambiguous, there was a high level of discomfort and a tendency to default to the box.

- When the *problem* was ambiguous and the *threat* was clear, fundamental debates about the mission of the Intelligence Community ensued.

This last tendency was particularly intriguing in that the discussions about the mission expanded to a sort of metaphysical dialogue about the purpose of intelligence in a democracy. For some, the world could be known – hard work and diligence would yield a pattern somewhere in the sifting process of intelligence. For others, the world was a place of illusions, filled with gray that could only be described.

In an awkward moment, like a marriage gone bad after 30 years, the two groups suddenly found themselves staring across the table at strangers.

Twenty-one miles to the south and west of Washington, D.C., at the outer edge of light pollution, the Bull Run battlefield stretches out in perfect isolation like a black carpet amid the growing suburban Manassas countryside. On a summer's night, standing near the spot where Stonewall Jackson got his famous nickname for holding back a Union charge, low on the southern horizon, you can see the constellation we know as Orion. No other constellation has so many bright stars – five are of second magnitude; two others of first magnitude. On the warrior's upraised right shoulder, poised to strike with his sword is the supergiant star Betelgeuse, 400 times the size of our sun. At his right foot, anchoring his stance is the bluish-white Rigel, smaller than our sun but 20,000 times brighter. The Great Orion Nebula, in which as many as 10,000 stars the size of our sun can fit, forms the blade of the sword.

Two thousand miles away, in northeastern Arizona, the same group of stars takes on a different image. For the Navaho of the high desert, these stars represent the Two Canoes, and – together with the constellations we know as Taurus, the Pleides, and Perseus higher up on the horizon – they form the Smoking Star, from which pipe smoke drifts lazily up to the Star-That-Never-Moves – our Polaris.

Perspective is everything. Not until late in the 19th century did science discover that the night sky has depth as well as breadth, that constellations not only are in the eye of the beholder, that they are distant illusions. By the early 20th century, when quantum physics wed astronomy, the illusion became deeper. However we characterize the apparent pattern of the clusters, the light we see in Manassas or Arizona takes about 400 years to reach us from the nearest star in the group. Each night in the sky, there appears an event that is already over. We are seeing the past in the present.

We can think of no better metaphor than *Starlight* to characterize the central problem for the Intelligence Community as it looks toward the future. Whether we examined the world of a criminal mastermind, of virulent disease, or a high-technology space race, the pattern of events in that world commonly turned on three characteristics: complexity, venues, and time – all of which can be captured in the metaphor of *Starlight*.

By complexity, we mean the word as used in Chaos Theory. Complexity, in this sense, is the developing scientific discipline that is based on the study of nonlinear systems. Both words – nonlinear and systems – are critical to understanding the theory.

A system is simply a way of understanding the relationship among things that interact. A brick wall, for example, is a simple, linear system whose interactions are based on how the bricks are laid. In theory at least, we can replicate the brick wall because we understand the interaction among the bricks, mortar, and gravity as a predictable system. Similarly, Newton's calculus – that bane of high school sophomores – is a system of mathematics that allows us to predict change within the context of straight linear functions.

Linear systems, such as calculus, can be *complicated*, but they are not *complex*. Complex systems are nonlinear. To understand their interactions, we must build models that approach the complexity of the systems themselves. The weather is complex: it can be effectively modeled only with an exact duplicate of itself.

In all of our five worlds, the interaction of billions of people, divergent cultures, altogether new kinds of power and new sources of wealth, coupled with chance, created genuinely *complex* outcomes. As a result, it quickly became clear that the predictability of our future worlds was far less than the past. The future is not Newtonian. To view it as such, to simplify it for the sake of easy analysis or presentation, is to risk missing its more subtle syncopation. To do that, we found, was to risk national security.

As a result, we came to view the events of the 20th century somewhat differently after *Proteus* than before. In the world of 1914, when Europe went to war in the trenches of Belgium and northern France, understanding both the origins of the war and the interaction of warriors and politicians was much easier than understanding conflict at the close of the century. This is not a facile observation about the proverbial value of hindsight, but rather an empirical appreciation derived from working in the future scenarios. Given a relatively smaller and less complex set of circumstances and actors (however *complicated* to those that experienced them in 1914) the events of World War I were inherently more predictable than those in the future appear to be.

We began to think about the last century's events less as a political and historical chronology and more as a transitional period from

(relatively) linear to nonlinear times. For us, the transitional period from 1914 to the fall of the Berlin Wall in 1989 was less
about world war or the demise of imperialism and communism
than a period in which the complexity of the world exploded as
the power and wealth of humans shifted from a local base to a
global one. It was a period in which the defining events and dominant players in the world moved from the relative linearity of
European political wars to the unpredictability of a planet where
multinational corporations; non-governmental organizations; ethnic, tribal, racial, and cultural subgroups; a hundred more nation
states; and a global media all interact.

This fundamental increase in complexity – and the need to sense
and understand the rhythms of the world differently tomorrow
than yesterday – arose as one of the most difficult intelligence
challenges in the future. Complexity is at the very center of what
the Intelligence Community will and will not be able to do – and
what technical and analytical tools it must develop and employ.
Ultimately, it speaks to the degree that the Community is able to
anticipate events at all in a non-Newtonian world. Complexity
reduces predictability, and in an increasingly unpredictable world,
the U.S. risks continuing strategic surprise.

§

The explosive increase in the complexity of *Protean* futures was
attended by a corresponding and fundamental change in our understanding of the venues in which the world's activities and enterprises were conducted. The arrival of global communications
and the undeniable impact of the Internet on the world was one

obvious new venue. There is much more to say about this in the coming chapters, especially in Chapter 9, where we describe a new way of thinking about the virtual world. In broader terms, however, cyberspace is but one of several new future venues, which taken collectively we came think about as "planes of influence," coining a 21st century expansion of the old Imperial term "spheres of influence".

To us, planes of influence came to represent those "places" in the future where friendly, hostile, or neutral actors might seek to influence others. In our informal taxonomy, built from the experience of the scenarios as played out by the workshop participants, the planes of influence in 2020 were:

- *Terrestrial.* The classic military and geopolitical domains of air, sea, undersea, and land, as well as the physical concentrations of wealth (*i.e.*, strategic sea lanes, oil fields);

- *Space.* The world of satellites (black and white) and future space platforms;

- *Spectral.* The electromagnetic spectrum in which so much of the electronic warfare, frequency management, and sensing occurs today and will occur in the future;

- *Virtual.* The global world of networks and connectivity;

- *Psychological.* Those media and conduits that can be used to influence the hearts and minds of people.

Our purpose in articulating these "planes of influence" is not to put forward a specific framework for a future Intelligence Community; rather, the categories arose *empirically* in the cataloging of the disparate events in several of the scenarios. Specifically, the categories were the product of the "outsider" workshop of non-intelligence professionals, who were more varied in professional background and experience than the "insiders."

For example, in the criminal mastermind scenario, *Militant Shangri-La,* most of the intelligence professionals agreed that the Alliance indeed posed a threat to the West. But for them, the central question was *intent* – they were sharply focused on what the Alliance was going to do next. Accustomed as they were, after a professional lifetime of fighting the Cold War, to focusing on the geopolitical and military aspects of hostile strategies, the intelligence professionals struggled, first to find a pattern, certain as they were, second, that there would surely *be* a pattern. For the "insiders", there was a presumption that intent, a group of actors, a mastermind, some preconceived plan, in fact existed, and the key object was to discover it. Their view of the events in the scenario was shaped not only by the certainty of intent but also by a tendency to focus on the traditional geopolitical venues and cyberspace. Somewhere in there lay the key to the code. But despite a week of working the problem, the group was never able to find the key they sought.

The "outsiders," who included business people, economists, environmentalists, and even poets, had a different struggle: it took much longer for them to agree that the Alliance *was*, in fact, a threat to the West. What some intelligence professionals saw as hostile Alliance propaganda, some "outsiders" saw as fair criticism. However, once the outsiders came to agree that the Alliance was hostile, they quickly devised the schema of the planes of influence listed above. In doing so, they gained insights that were missed by the professionals.

First, in analyzing the scenario across all the planes of influence, the outsiders simply found more Alliance actions in the scenario, which to the insiders had either gone unnoticed or were discarded as irrelevant in classical terrestrial venues.

Second, by looking across all the actions in all the venues, the outsiders saw a pattern that had eluded the insiders: the Alliance strategy, in classical Western eyes almost nonsensical, was simply to keep the West constantly at the edge of social, political, and economic chaos. In this view, the Alliance intent was not a strategic object per se, which the insiders sought to find, but rather a strategic condition: in keeping the West reactive – dancing on a string of seemingly unrelated events in the media, on the seas, in space and in the spectrum – the Alliance sought unspecified opportunity.

As we observed in the previous discussion of complexity, looking for linearity leads to strategic surprise. Here, we saw the same consequence: a failure to appreciate the totality of the new venues for activity in the future left the U.S. on the strategic defensive. The Alliance had succeeded in seizing strategic initiative from the West. Perhaps even more worrisome was that a strategy of opportunism led to a cycle of events in which the West was goaded, then reacted, and the Alliance goaded again, in response to the Western reaction. Like a martial artist, the Alliance was using the West's own weight to keep it off balance. The pattern of intent the insiders sought was its own reaction. Thus, viewed from the perspective of the West, the pattern of activity was not discernable. The Alliance set up the U.S. and its allies to be their own stimulus; no matter how the West reacted to an event, the Alliance could move to keep chaos abroad on the planet. Despite its enormous strength, and its ability to tactically take the offensive, the Alliance succeeded in confining the West to the strategic defensive. In this way, the weaker hamstring outdid the stronger.

Once the events were placed across a set of planes of influence, however, the workshop participants began to find new tools. Sidebar discussions on the present Arab-Israeli conflicts, the Central African tribal wars, and the Colombian insurgency ensued, in which the concrete organizational structure, like the view of the night sky from Arizona and Manassas, led to different explanations of the same phenomena. Appreciative as we all are of the importance of perspective in everyday life, here we found some examples of how organizational perspective leads to blindness.

§

The final component of the *Starlight* phenomenon was time. Though we are conditioned these days to think of time as a shrinking commodity in an ever-busier world, in the scenarios, time was a factor of much more subtle interplay. The causal factor was the widespread interconnectivity of the worlds, which persistently and spontaneously arose even when we deliberately tried to invent scenarios in which global connectivity was minimized. Like the trend toward a global economy, the momentum of an increasingly wired world was difficult to turn around.

So strong was the tendency for the workshops to find a need for connectivity in every world, that a deliberate attempt on the part of the scenario authors to write it out of the future worlds became almost artificial. In *Amazon.plague*, for example, where fear of betraying personal health data when using the Internet was omnipresent in the population, it nonetheless became the central tool in strategies to control the disease. In *The Enemy Within*, where walled communities proliferated for protection, it became the principal pathway for social intercourse. In *Yankee Going Home*, paradoxically, global connectivity was the only way an isolationist country could remain relevant and stay competitive in a global economy.

If the history of our species to date is conquering the physical space of the planet, we found that the technology of the new, wired world has opened up new opportunities to control time. This observation had ominous implications, as well, and presented yet another risk of surprise to the Intelligence Community.

The ability to orchestrate events across the physical, virtual, spectral, and psychological venues in sequence or in parallel made it possible to influence opinion and to create and manage perception on an unprecedented scale. In today's world, we see the inklings of this ability already: the timing of press releases, of diplomatic actions, of corporate mergers and earnings are all-important in creating impact. Just as a shaped charge increases the effective force in munitions, timing shapes consequences of planned events.

In a world where complexity and new venues complicate the intelligence problems, time also can be an ally. In all of our worlds, the global balance of political, economic, military and cultural power was quickly and significantly altered. In some cases, the catalyst took a familiar form: a dramatic and obvious event. In others, subtle, incremental and seemingly unrelated occurrences in multiple planes of influence combined to create change.

Often in our workshops, the sequencing of events revealed the only discernable patterns. For the insiders in *Militant Shangri-La*, it was not enough to catalog the discrete actions of the Alliance across all the planes of influence. Alliance opportunism could only be perceived when the disparate special events were placed on a timeline. Only then did the rhythm of the Alliance's action-reaction-action cycle emerge clearly.

In the *Protean* futures, deliberately timed events were easy to see, but they were only part of the temporal cacophony. The natural acceleration of global enterprises resulting from the wired world was much harder to understand. Economic transaction flows instantaneously defined and redefined wealth and power. The ability – intended or unintended – of the media to shape perception and, in some cases *to define* perception, was vastly increased by ubiquitous communication. Indeed, as we explore in Chapter 5, time has a real impact on the very concepts of truth and falsehood.

§

For the Intelligence Community, the phenomenon we call *Starlight*, with its components of complexity, venue, and time, poses a set of formidable technical and operational challenges. We think the implications can be summarized in the following way:

- Foresight and uncertainty management become the objects of the intelligence cycle in the future;

- The task for the Intelligence Community, therefore, is not merely the cataloging of events, but more the recognition of patterns. As a result, given finite resources, sensors may be less important than new ways to analyze complex data;

- Pattern finding is, in part, a function of expertise. In the future, the Intelligence Community needs expertise in economics, organizational theory, psychology, network topology, and complexity mathematics – to name a few;

- If pattern-finding techniques are successful, it is possible that the Intelligence Community can afford to miss some events and still understand threats. However, patterns are not only harder to find than events, they are harder to prove;

- Time is often the analytical nexus among seemingly disparate events across multiple planes of influence. A sophisticated understanding of time and timing is essential to creation of an Intelligence Community that can deliver indications and warnings, both strategic and tactical, to future leaders;

- Finally, reactive postures – getting behind the timeline – leave one vulnerable and sow the seeds of false security.

Zaire, that vast central river basin that drains the Congo River, may be the most troubled country in the world. Blessed with some of the most beautiful scenery in Africa, three-quarters of it are still jungle and woodland. Rising in elevation gradually across 1200 miles from the Atlantic to Lake Tanganyika in the eastern mountains, Zaire (actually, the "former" Zaire: once the Belgian Congo, the Congo, and Zaire, and it has been since 1997 the Democratic Republic of Congo) is one of the world's great mining repositories. Much of country's troubles stem from fights over its copper, diamond and cobalt mines in the eastern province of Katanga. Since the mid-1980s, Western business interests have funded powerful corporate "security forces" that have variously battled and embraced government and rebel troops alike in a complex civil war. More trouble comes from the ravages of tribal warfare in the neighboring countries to the east across the Lake: Uganda, Rwanda, Burundi, and Tanzania, where Hutus and Tutsis are engaged in mutual genocide.

All the while, the AIDS epidemic is ravaging Zaire and her neighbors. Sub-Saharan Africa contains more than two-thirds of all the people living with HIV in the world—nearly 21 million men, women and children — and fully 83 percent of the world's AIDS deaths. Four out of five HIV-positive women in the world live in central and southern Africa, as do 87 percent of the infected children. There is no evidence the epidemic is slowing.

To the north and east, in Sudan, in the midst of drought and famine, food is the critical need. But for Zairians, there is a different need. In that country, the most valuable commodity is *Sanctuary*. For workers in the Katanga mines, sanctuary means avoiding AIDS tests (and, with it, treatment) to hide evidence of infection. Those who are infected have little chance of keeping a job, much less having a future, in the mining industry. To the north, sanctuary for nearly a million refugees means fleeing into Zaire to escape the murderous Hutu-Tutsi fighting. For businessmen in Kinshasa, once the thriving, sophisticated Belgian Congo capital Leopoldville, sanctuary means finding somewhere outside the country to hide their wealth. Zaire's economy has crashed since the mid-1980s and is now experiencing an inflation rate of 147 per cent.

Nor is it just Zaire where sanctuary, in one form or another, is in demand. In all five of our *Protean* futures, we found one of our most remarkable counter-intuitions: the more the world opens, the more it closes. For the Intelligence Community today, denied access is a very real concern; tomorrow it is worse. We recognize that one of the downsides of an increasing worldwide high-technology base is the enhanced ability of hostile powers to hide information that has traditionally been of high intelligence interest.

To that end, this concern has been focused on just that—traditionally valuable information. In the worlds of *Proteus*, we found a much more pervasive and much harder set of problems surrounding "hiding and finding." To capture the larger trend, we called these future issues the "problem" of *Sanctuary*. After seeing *Sanctuary* manifest itself in the future, we were able to look back upon today with different eyes, where we could see some of the multiple dimensions of hiding and finding.

- Inside the European Central Bank, for example, the delay and general dearth of data on the European economies places it far behind its American counterpart. America is 29 days quicker at bringing out employment data; 44 days quicker with industrial production; and 103 days ahead on hourly wages. Much of the problem lies in the unwillingness of European member banks to share the data with the ECB in an effort to hide the secrets of their own economic database;[1]

- In the southern Nevada desert lays the famed Area 51 at Nellis Air Force Base. Shrouded in secrecy for decades, this is where UFO enthusiasts have long suspected the U.S. government of hiding aliens. Earlier this year, the first commercial one-meter resolution imaging satellite flew over the base, and images were sold publicly. Around the world, on the drawing board or the launching pad, similar imaging satellites are in queue in the U.S., Russia, Japan, Israel, and South Korea. "Not so long ago, it seems, nations were able to hide their armaments, misdeeds and fortresses from the eyes of nosy civilians, while the militaries could pry into most corners of the globe from spy satellites, knowing they could control who could take a peek. ...No more," observed the *New York Times* in its story on the incident;[2]

- In China, parents who have flouted the government's two-children restriction are hiding their children;

- California winemakers are using satellite images to create a "vegetation index" that tells them when grapes have reached optimal ripeness;

- In Washington state, an adopted child, now grown and searching for her biological mother, is seeking to change the law that withholds the mother's identity;

- In 1999, the Securities and Exchange Commission slapped huge fines on some upstart companies which allegedly have doctored their corporate books in order to hide earnings statistics;

- The U.S. Census Bureau's angst at both individual and congressional attempts to thwart carrying out its survey this year was the subject of widespread media attention.

At length a fuller pattern emerged that betrayed a kind of increasing voltage abroad in the modern world – a growing urge to hide and an increasing global ability to find. Just as the problem of *Starlight* exploded the complexity of the venues in which the future Intelligence Community must look, *Sanctuary* implies not only new places to hide but also more places to hide.

In our parlance, there is a duality to the idea of *Sanctuary*. Wherever we found a propensity to hide in the future, we found a parallel development in ways and techniques to find. Indeed, in several of the worlds, a whole new marketplace developed across the globe in which the practitioners of security did a land office business which, in turn, sparked a technology race in what we might call *Sanctuary* and counter-*Sanctuary* technologies and techniques. For security experts, from cryptologists guarding the data or guards patrolling the perimeters, the open world of 2020 is a land of opportunity. *Sanctuary* is big business.

And, *Sanctuary* takes many forms. In our future worlds, the workshop participants cataloged the following informal list of potentially intrusive activities from which or for which *Sanctuary* was sought:

- Self-protection
- Civil rights
- Information warfare attacks
- Epidemiology
- Genetic information
- Border security
- Crime
- Institutional penetration
- Economic intelligence
- Weapons of mass destruction
- Pollution
- Threats to the food chain
- Mass migration

For the Intelligence Community, the phenomenon we call *Sanctuary*, with its duality, its emerging marketplace and new technologies, and its global presence, we think the implications are these:

- From private citizens to non-governmental organizations, from corporations to nation states, the future will be an increasingly secretive place;

- *Sanctuary* will be extremely valuable in every aspect of public and private life, and it will be pursued as the antidote to an invasive world: "Life, liberty, the pursuit of happiness, and leave me alone;"

- New venues for denial will arise at least as fast as the instruments of surveillance;

- The things the Intelligence Community must find in 2020 may not be physical or even virtual. Some, such as information and the instantaneous manifestation of wealth, will be temporal in nature. There was evidence, nonetheless, that all might leave trails;

- Both discrete and broad events will be hidden by sanctuary;

- Certain conditions, such as the emergence of a knowledge-based economy, high mobility, blurred sovereignty, and confused loyalties, will lead to an inability to understand others' sense of what is valuable;

- Off-the-shelf denial technologies will be accessible to most. Global expertise in technologies that provide sanctuary will increase;

- At the same time, the public will be less tolerant of intrusion and more suspicious of intelligence activities;

- Finally, not knowing what you do not know complicates intelligence priorities by orders of magnitude. *Sanctuary* exacerbates this. No doubt, the Intelligence Community will have to work harder to gain intelligence.

As every fly fisherman knows, catching trout happens in a different world than the one we experience in our everyday lives. For most of us, the workday occurs in a cultural and sociological cauldron, where human interactions dominate, and bad weather is often the only reminder of the colossal forces of nature that are ongoing in the background of our lives. Rest yourself for a moment, and daydream of a trout stream – say in the highest mountains of Nepal.

For the last 150 million years, the irresistible Indian subcontinent has been ramming itself against the immovable central Asian landmass and gaining at about one centimeter a year. One result is Mount Everest. Down from the massive mountainside, the rivers rush onward until, inevitably, they drop through rock riffles exposed in the erosion of the streambed. Just after each of these miniature waterfalls, the water slows and swirls, bringing with it food for the innumerable species that live in the resulting pool.

Each pool is a distinct ecosystem in which the life forms experience the physical world as the point at which fluid layers intersect. For the trout, the mayflies, and the other species, the workaday life beneath the mountain occurs in the three inches directly above and below the surface of the water – where the H_2O molecules are in the constant Brownian movement to maintain a very complex chemical equilibrium. Look closer and there is a point where water and water vapor coexist in equal parts. Closer still, and the forces gripping the atoms can be experienced. Even closer are the individual electrons but, as the German quantum physicist Werner Heisenberg revealed in 1926, this point is where our understanding of the physical world breaks down. All we can know is a set of probabilities that the electron is in one place or another. Press on deeper, and the world becomes a set of six bizarre quarks, each spinning in different directions.

All of this knowledge–save perhaps the importance of casting the right fly into the right six-inch fluid interface–human beings have learned in the past 100 years. In a century of incredible discoveries, none is perhaps more remarkable than the simultaneity of the great and small. Literally, Everest is there because small things matter. The discovery of quantum mechanics has led us to understand truly mind-boggling relationships–the relationships among time and space, black holes, and string theory to name a few. The discovery of tectonic plates has taught us that nothing on this planet stands still.

In our work with *Proteus*, we found that the 20th century discoveries about simultaneity–small stuff impacting big stuff, to put it more simply – continued in the future. These discoveries not only reveal remarkable insights into the physical and biological worlds, but also, like the fluid interface on the trout stream, cause the distinction between the real and virtual worlds to pale.

In particular, across all of our worlds it was clear that instruments of power and sources of threat in the future would come in smaller and smaller packages–but with no lessening in lethality. Biological viruses, sophisticated software agents, and all varieties of nanotechnologies are good examples. Even today we can see each of these "small things" having dramatic impacts on events of the present world: the recent "love bug" computer virus, the discovery among residents of a small Italian town of a new human blood protein that can prevent heart disease, the proliferation of micro-machines in medicine and manufacturing.

In the future, we saw not only more, but also different possibilities for *Small Stuff* along two general paths of development.

First, there is the continuing evolutionary development of these technologies. Cloning of biological entities is likely to continue, and the technologies and knowledge base needed to accomplish cloning are not likely to be limited to a few countries or corporations. The scientific cat is out of the bag and, for better or worse, cloning seems poised to become a worldwide capability. Similarly, millions of people are now engaged in the development of software. Tomorrow there will be tens of millions, all working in a highly competitive marketplace. Innovation and rapid iteration are the likely results.

Beyond the evolutionary developments, however, we caught glimpses of a stunning realization. Where the worlds of digital mathematics, electronics, biotechnology, and nanotechnology met, our traditional definitions of each—perhaps even of life itself—tended to give way. At the nexus of these disciplines, there is a sort of technological Zen: what else is a gene but a digital database? Moreover, as our knowledge of *Small Stuff* expands, such statements have truth beyond just analogy. Indeed, the amino acid pairs in DNA are essentially chemical capacitors, albeit with a different molecular structure than in a silicon or gallium chip.

We suspect that biologists who use macro-definitions to differentiate living organisms from inert objects—a view that holds true from atop the Everest peaks—are due for major disciplinary overhaul. Beyond where the mayflies meet the trout—that is, where electrons are probabilities—what is understood to be "alive" and what is not might not hold. Indeed, we may find all kinds of life around us that we had not noticed. Armed with a new and broader definition, we might conclude that new life forms are possible, and—like matter and energy—that these life forms may have different states—in this case biological, digital, micro-mechanical, or all three.

§

For the Intelligence Community, *Small Stuff* — nanotechnology plus biotechnology plus cybertechnology—is a double-edged sword that will create both opportunities and threats. At once, it will be the key to exploring all of the venues of *Starlight*, and it is the key to both sides of *Sanctuary*—penetrating denied areas and sustaining covertness.

Small Stuff almost certainly will lead to a wholesale redefinition of what sensors are, and it probably will point toward new venues for technical exploration. In a future world in which *Small Stuff* plays big roles, sensors that can measure genetic mutation rates, platelets passing through arterial constrictions, photons across fiber optic gates, and click-throughs at investment sites on the web will be as relevant and necessary as those that help us count an adversary's tank barrels.

At the same time, cyber-, bio- and nanotechnologies seem likely to create a whole new environment for deception and destruction. Consider an easily imagined future capability: transporting the digital data that defines the genome of a malignant virus across a future Internet. Inherent in that act is the transformation of the essential information of life from one state to another (biological to digital to biological again). From there, the idea of biological encryption is a small step, and Star Trek's transporter starts to look like just another supercomputer problem.

We believe the Intelligence Community should be concerned about how the cyber-, bio- and nanotechnologies will change its customers. On one hand, the armed forces are becoming smaller and more high-tech every day. Both the Air Force and the Army have declared their intent to change the size, doctrine, and command structures of its deploying forces. The Army, which is presently exploring a move from divisions to brigades as its principal operational component, will have entirely new intelligence and dissemination requirements based simply on structural change. And all of the Services will experience dramatically faster decision cycles as information technologies erode the classical hierarchical command structures of the past. Differential applications of *Small Stuff* will create extremely complex C^2 problems – for friend and foe alike.

We also believe that "smaller" may not mean "cheaper." One of the most important questions for the Intelligence Community to examine is whether the *Small Stuff* technologies it needs are likely to be developed largely in the private marketplace (as information technology is today) or if government-sponsored research and development will be necessary. If the latter proves to be the case, many of the highly touted commercial trends of today's defense procurement—best business practices, indefinite quantity contracting, off-the-shelf procurement, and so on—may become problematic when the government has different technology needs than the marketplace. Regarding acquisition, it is difficult to tell whether the Intelligence Community of the future will have more in common with the government-fueled aerospace industry of the 1950s or the global information technology market of the 1990s.

Finally, the arrival of small technologies will make co-location of the sensing *and* analytic functions possible. Over the past 15 years, an increasing ability to conduct processing near the sensors has made tactical intelligence more and more time-sensitive. The arrival of very small technologies will accelerate this trend and perhaps alter the ways in which the "take" are disseminated and analyzed. In short, it seemed clear that *Small Stuff* brings with it big change, not the least of which will be a fundamental change in the intelligence cycle itself, with attendant impacts in time, resources, capability, and efficiency.

W e're guessing, of course, but our best understanding of the development of human language is that it was not invented until after the last Ice Ages, some 10,000 years ago, and long after the demise of the Neanderthals. Writing began some seven millennia later, though notches on bone or wood batons seem to have been an early effort to count sheep— whether to sleep or not, we'll never know.

For thousands of years, then, human knowledge was passed down by word of mouth or by direct experience in a largely natural world. Our earliest known Western poetry, Homer's *Iliad* and *Odyssey*, were composed in a form to be recited, and more to the point, to be remembered by generations of recitors without the benefit of the written word to recall their lines. There must have been many Homers and many epics between the Ice Age and the development of writing, but only Homer's have survived.

It is difficult to imagine the intellectual frameworks for such knowledge. How did early Man come to separate sheep from goats, as it were? The inevitable human process of compartmentalization is a construct of reality that is lost to us now. Whole taxonomies of objects and natural phenomena must have been devised and passed from generation to generation, most made obsolete by the onset of agriculture and cities. All that was truly ancient was lost in the technological revolution of Cuneiform writing and the scritch-scratch of the stylus. What little residue we have of that *weltanschauung* is the magnificent cave art of Western Europe and a growing collection of crude "Venus" figurines uncovered across Eurasia.

In whatever way these ancient peoples saw themselves and the world around them, most anthropologists agree they were as "modern" physiologically and intellectually as we are today. However they conveyed the knowledge they acquired, and the manner in which knowledge arose for them, was the same as it is for us. For untold millennia, epistemology has held that knowledge arises from three sources:

- From authority (the leader says it is true)

- From empiricism (the mammoth is bigger than I am)

- From revelation (God says it is true)

Proteus showed us a number of frightening prospects, but none more shocking or perplexing than the possibility that, for the first time in human experience, a fourth kind of knowledge may be arising. In our work, we found that the use of complex, interconnected global networks can lead to the spontaneous creation of knowledge. This discovery is significant for two reasons:

- First, the speed with which new knowledge was created and disseminated in our worlds was nothing short of remarkable.

- Second, the new knowledge was silent on intrinsic truth or falsehood.

In other words, we were startled to discover that what was demonstrably true could become demonstrably false if enough people believed in it, and if the knowledge moved across the globe fast enough. Thus, knowledge in our worlds took on a set of changeable "states" that were mutable in a wired world.

We struggled as a group to understand *Veracity*, recognizing as we did the implications to the Intelligence Community. In the end, we could grasp it only by example and metaphor. Some of us came to understand *Veracity* in terms of knowledge and anti-knowledge − a parallel with the ideas in physics of matter and antimatter. For others, the best examples were from economics: the idea that if favorable (or unfavorable) information on a company circulated far and fast enough, it might become true even if the information was completely fabricated. There is, however, a subtlety to this example that belies its initial clarity. Unlike propaganda or deception, with which we have much experience, here the illusion actually becomes reality. That is a horse of a different color! The more we explored *Veracity*, the more complicated it became, so we cast about for more examples to help ourselves understand it.

The German novel *Jakob the Liar* [3] illustrates Veracity to a "T". Two Jewish friends in the midst of the Warsaw ghetto are laboring to load a train when one, Mischa, in a berserk moment, readies himself to attack a Nazi sentry. To stop him, Jakob suddenly grabs him and tells the Great Lie, one sure to gain the immediate attention of a news-starved and desperate people:

> "I have a radio!" says Jakob.
> It's not the sentries who have fired. …Jakob has fired a bullet straight to the heart. …Mischa sits there motionless: the Russians are two hundred and fifty miles from here, near someplace called Bezanika, and Jakob has a radio…
>
> Jakob gets up; they can't sit there indefinitely. He is angrier than ever. He has been forced to launch irresponsible claims, and it's that ignorant idiot who has just forced him… He'll tell Mischa the truth all right, not this minute but sometime today… Within an hour in fact, an hour at most, maybe even sooner, he'll tell the truth. Let the fellow enjoy a few more carefree minutes…

But Jakob never does, and by nightfall the rumor is going around the ghetto that hope is on the way. In that way, false hopes lead to true hopefulness.

When we looked for them, there were many examples in the everyday news. The one quoted below describes a remarkable event in which Congress moved to squelch a rumor that it was taking action on Internet taxes (see inset pg. 44).

The problem of translating poetry, particularly from oriental texts, also gave us some insight into *Veracity* and the art of understanding what is knowable. In the eighth century, Chinese poetry reached its zenith in the T'ang Dynasty with the masterful lines of Tu Fu. The originals are composed, of course, in Chinese characters and in a style that deliberately leaves much to the native reader's imagination. The first two lines of one of his most well known compositions, *Thinking of My Younger Brother on a Moonlit Night*, consists of five character sounds, which translate at their simplest as:

Shù	Guard
Gŭ	Drums
Dwàn	Cut off
Rén	People's
Syíng	Travel

When the poem is translated, however, the meaning shifts with the perspective of the translating poet. Here is Canadian poet Greg Whincup's translation:

> Drums on the watchtower[4]
> Cut off men's travels

And the German, Witter Bynner:

> A wanderer hears drums portending battle.[5]

Well, precisely. Which is it, war or not? At length, these two translations seemed to capture in a poetic metaphor another dimension of the problem of *Veracity*, one that we mentioned briefly in our introductory chapter: what is the role of the Intelligence Community in determining "truth?"

During the "insiders" workshop, significant debate arose not only about the Community's core mission, but also – on an almost metaphysical plane – whether the world, in fact, was knowable. For not a few – and to the surprise of the rest – the world was indeed knowable, if not quantifiable, and the mission of the Intelligence Community was to be the "arbiter of truth," a phrase that stunned the opposing, more philosophical camp. In one instance, a very senior former intelligence officer left one of the workshops after making the point that U.S. intelligence inevitably would "know"

Congress to Block Imaginary Internet Tax Bill

By Peter S. Goodman
Washington Post Staff Writer
Wednesday, May 10, 2000; Page E01

Not unlike word of black helicopters floating overhead, the report filtered through the Internet: Washington was about to act on nefarious legislation that would tax the use of the global computer system.

"One congressman, Tony Schnell, has even suggested a twenty to forty dollar a month surcharge on all internet service," warned a writer on an Internet discussion group called alt.government.abuse, imploring others to flood Capitol Hill with email in opposition. "Don't sit by and watch your freedoms erode away! Just say 'NO!' to Bill 602-P."

Never mind that there is no Congressman Schnell. Nor is there a House Bill 602-P. As the rumor spread, a flood of email indeed arrived. And even after the hoax was revealed, the electronic wave it spawned continued to reverberate.

In the age of the Internet, even a prank can alter political reality.[6]

---

what had gone on in the ensuing years from the present to the scenarios of 2020. So, any vagary was, in his view, unlikely. "We would know it," he said.

He was not alone, and this is not surprising. In fact, it is chipped in stone in the marble foyer of the CIA's Original Headquarters Building:

And ye shall know the truth,
and the truth shall make you free
John 8 :32

The idea of *Veracity*, its nature, and its achievement in the pursuit of intelligence collection is a core issue. Not only did we find the frightening prospect of new kinds of knowledge divorced from either truth or falsehood, but also we uncovered a fundamental fissure in the bedrock of the Intelligence Community's view of itself. Beyond those, we found still more implications, with which we close our chapter, still unsettled in its ideas:

- When knowledge takes on intrinsic value in the globally net-worked world, unintended consequences may result. Under certain conditions, something that is incorrect or false can become an accepted truth. Therein lay the seeds of illusion, deception, and above all, change.

- Whether knowledge arises from a deliberate attack or from the innocent creation of false impressions from mismatched perceptions, knowledge will become one of the most power-ful and frightening forces in a globally networked world.

- When coupled with shifting 21st century loyalties and the real-ity of global perception management, knowledge will make vast and permanent change possible in short order.

- If, in a world of instantaneous networks, what is false can become true, and what is true can become false, the very con-cept of ground truth is dangerously limiting.

- In the progression from data through knowledge to insight, understanding what is knowable may be more important than differentiating between truth and falsehood.

- It may still be necessary for the Intelligence Community to count specific entities (*e.g.*, tanks and ICBM silos). However, if that approach drives the effort to understand a complex, networked, multiplane future, then significant threats will be missed.

- Some people have a need for truth (whether it exists or not), and someone will strive to profit from being the "arbiter of truth" in the future. Nonetheless, in a complex world, ambiguity is a constant companion and an instrument of power.

- Notwithstanding the philosophical schism noted above, the Intelligence Community may be better poised to deal with the ideas of *Veracity* than business, where, in the end, it is the bottom-line truth that matters.

For all of its fame, Thomas Jefferson's Monticello is a surprisingly small place. The restless mind of one of America's greatest intellectuals never allowed his home to be finished. In the end, after 40 years of designing and redesigning the house, Jefferson shoehorned 33 rooms into a mere 11,000 square feet atop Carter Mountain near Charlottesville, Virginia. Modest, for a mansion!

The immediate grounds are also close. On three sides, Monticello's lawn drops off sharply to peaceful overlooks. In Virginia, where all four seasons are distinct, Jefferson could look out of his hand-blown glass windows toward the distant Blue Ridge and literally watch the months and years go by.

On the fourth side, however, the views are less pacific. Literally a stone's throw from the President's famous study, with its ingenious inventions and his beloved books, are the cabins of the slaves who built his home. Across the lawn and beyond the vegetable garden, the rows of cabins were built in perfect alignment – dirt paths between rows of wooden cells. Whether through the blown glass windows of the mansion or the open squares of the cabin walls, it was impossible not to take notice of each other. And while the Great Man read Newton, Descartes, Bacon and Locke in his study, other men spent lifetimes working in wood, stone, brick and the land itself.

Like Washington's Mount Vernon, Monticello is a superb example of New World labor imitating Old World style and grace: it is, in every sense, an artifact.

Jefferson himself tried to embody thoughts and ideas born in the Old World. Yet, mesmerized as he was by the thoughts and ideas of the Enlightenment's philosophers and scientists, he could not enlighten himself to the realities around him. Ironically, as he crafted the ideas and sentences that became the ideals of the United States...

> We hold these truths to be self-evident, that all men are created equal, that they are endowed by their Creator with certain un-alienable Rights, that among these are Life, Liberty, and the pursuit of Happiness.

...he remained blind to the plight of the men and women who actually built Monticello. It would be three more generations before Jefferson's beloved Enlightenment finally reached American shores, when Abraham Lincoln signed the Emancipation Proclamation and made the Civil War a moral combat.

In the last decade in particular, Jefferson's complex character has been the subject of a number of new studies, including the scientific examinations of the DNA of the descendents of one of Jefferson's house slaves, Sally Hemmings. They seem to prove the rumors of the relationship between the two. And so we are left to wonder at a man who could conceive of liberty for an entire nation, but could not grant it to those he loved. What are we to think?

We can consider two things in thinking about Jefferson, at least. One, of course, is the nature of his personal blindness—how can such a man live with such personal contradictions? It is difficult to understand, and not a few biographers have struggled to explain it. But in the end, no matter how deeply into Jefferson's personality we explore, there are few lessons for the rest of us. Jefferson simply is a mystery.

There is another consideration brought to mind by Jefferson's paradoxes, however, that is far more relevant to us: the lesson that the routine of a secure life blinds us to the certain revolution that follows when the existing world collides head-on with a broad, new set of ideas. Jefferson could grasp *ideas* on the move, but he simply could not envision their ultimate *effect*.

The lesson Jefferson's paradox provides for us is that his blindness is not unique. All around us in the post-Cold War environment, there are emerging ideas, the seeds of genuine revolutions. Some are benign; others, no doubt, much less so. We must look carefully about, outside all of the windows, to see change and not be satisfied with the view that is most comfortable.

In our time, empire is still colliding with independence, secularism with spiritualism, environmentalists with capitalists, feminists with chauvinists, pro-abortion with pro-life — on and on and on. We see it on the news every day. All over the world, men and women are on collision courses with established ideas. The only things that are changing faster than the technologies of the world are the people of the world. Again, as in Jefferson's time, people everywhere are on the move, propelled by new ideas. And, in our increasingly wired world, both the speed and the impact of the impending collision are likely to increase.

In the *Protean* worlds of 2020, we saw no signs that the rate of change diminished. People and ideas were on the move everywhere. In the plague-ridden world, *Amazon.plague*, people came to value far different commodities than in the past. New kinds of communities arose, and the world divided into those at risk and those not at risk. New manifestations of wealth emerged, health and privacy not the least among them. In the domestically fractionalized world, *The Enemy Within*, physical security and ideological disputes led to enclaves. The rise of a global media network wedded to a sham environmentalism in *Militant Shangri-la* lead to the creation of a huge new banking empire as tens of millions of people across the world poured their savings into the idealism of the "Earth Network."

As we considered those worlds, it became possible for us to look "back" at the year 2000 with a different viewpoint. The seeds of a new kind of atlas began to germinate in our minds as we observed how people and ideas moved. Physical and geopolitical representations of the planet clearly were inadequate to capture the diversity we saw. What we needed was a whole new approach to synthesizing the human activity and the physical phenomena of the world. *Proteus* showed us that neither a classical map nor one-meter resolution images could give us adequate understanding of the world. Staring at those images was like looking at the Blue Ridge from Jefferson's windows; they gave us little inkling, no understanding, no warning of the foment visible from the cabin view.

After we had looked at some of the possibilities of 2020, we could see today differently. We were not omniscient; we didn't gain hindsight. Rather, through the *Proteus* experience we became accustomed to looking out all of the windows, not just some. Examples of human *Herds* on the move then became easy to find.

The idea, for example, that millions of Chinese would come together in a cult–the Falun Gong–that combined breathing exercises with a cosmology that promises a saved person could literally fly into paradise was still strange, but its emergence was less surprising.

We found them in Birmingham, England, the birthplace of the Industrial Revolution, where the Labor Party is beginning to lose its traditional foothold to the Justice for Kashmiri Community Party (JFK). Birmingham is now home to 100,000 Muslims of Kashmiri origin – about 10 percent of the population. The JFK, originally founded as a protest against continuing imprisonment in Britain of two Kashmiri separatists for the killing of an Indian diplomat, has become Britain's most successful ethnically-based party, threatening Labor's long cherished aims as the party of racial minorities and the poor.[7]

Twelve hundred miles to the east, the population of Riga, Latvia, is dividing along different lines. When Moscow ruled the Baltics, the "Red Riflemen" who fought the Nazis on the side of the Red Army were the official heroes. They were honored with Hero of Lenin awards, regaled in the newspapers, and celebrated on patriotic holidays. "Legionnaires"–those who sided with the Nazis against the communists–were outcasts. Suspect in the eyes of communist officials after the war, they were tried and, if permitted to live, assigned the lowest of jobs. Now the historical table has turned, and it is Soviet partisans who are being investigated for war crimes. For the past year, veterans of Nazi-formed units have taken to the streets, holding parades and singing about how the "party" is over for the Russians.[8]

At length we came to recognize that the emerging power and influence of non-traditional organizations matters far less than the underlying movement of people and ideas – how people see themselves and their place in the world financially, socially, and spiritually. In each of the *Protean* worlds, the intersection of changes in such forces as demographics, economics, and technology led to the creation of influential transnational and sub-national groups that reshaped how people viewed their loyalties. In those futures, the loyalties and affinities that bind people to organizations and groups–corporations, religions, gated enclaves, factions or advocacy groups–are complex and dynamic.

In particular, across the worlds, we found three common themes:

- That the sheer number of identities and loyalties an individual possessed increased, with a concurrent tendency toward confliction. Schizophrenia of a sort set in for many.

- That in an open world of instantaneous information exchange where perception changes rapidly, skittishness among groups became apparent. Already torn by multiple loyalties, the presence of powerfully presented ideas was almost always persuasive.

- That, for some, the reaction to complexity was not schizophrenia but deep entrenchment. For these people, continuity dictated extremely narrow and rigid loyalties that shifted only under extreme pressure.

For the Intelligence Community, there were three central implications of the phenomenon we call *Herds*. First, in three of the worlds, it became very clear that the Community's public reputation as a forthright arbiter of truth not only mattered; it became central to its effectiveness. Second, intelligence leaders will have to think a lot more about people and how people view themselves in the future than they do today. *Power*, as we shall see in Chapter 8, arises from values. Finally, the conflicting loyalties of the *Protean* populations made it very difficult to retain high-quality, multidisciplinary talent. This difficulty, as we will see in *Bedfellows* in Chapter 10, may become a central challenge to the Intelligence Community.

In the last several years, anthropologists have come to agree that hominids arose out of Africa not just once, but multiple times, beginning as early as 7 million years ago. It is a recent consensus that has ended decades of scientific argument over whether fossils found in the Orient and Australia and those found in Africa represent independent origins of our species. In the end, microbiology resolved the mystery. It now seems most likely that our beginnings can be traced to the Great Rift Valley, a huge gash in the landscape that runs south from Jordan through modern Ethiopia, Kenya and Tanzania. With its dramatic highlands, forested plateaus, and precipitous slopes that plunge 3000 feet to hot, dry lowlands, it is everything we tourists imagine when we think of Africa. The Serengeti, the cataracts of the Nile, and Mount Kilimanjaro are all part of this same system.

The geological emergence of the valley had two effects that were keys to the development of our species. First, it posed a formidable east-west barrier to animal populations, effectively isolating our ancestors from their ancestors, which limited the breeding population and created a genetic cauldron for evolutionary change. At the same time, the Rift created new ecological conditions. Eventually, arboreal creatures – apes – dominated the areas west of the barrier. To the east, where savannah arose, new approaches were needed, and so, to make a long story short, here we are.

Exactly how many times hominid species arose from and left the valley is a different mystery. What we *do* know with certainty, however, is that the pathway was out of Africa were always the same. Geography dictates it: north along the Nile. And once out of the Nile Delta, you have to turn right: the narrow strip of land along the Mediterranean coast of modern Israel, Lebanon, and Syria is the only land route from Egypt. It is no surprise, then, that ancient history (and no doubt pre-history) is replete with wars and woes all along the way. It is one of those places where history does seem to repeat itself. Megiddo, where 30,000 Egyptians and Hittites battled over control of a pass in the second millennium B.C.E. is an hour's drive from the Israeli positions on the modern Golan Heights.

This area is also the part of the world where trade and agriculture both began. It is in the walled oasis city of Jericho, one of mankind's first cities, where we find the first signs of agriculture (circa 8,000 B.C.E.) in the mutated seeds of naturally occurring Triticum wheat. Here also are the cities of Byblos and Ugarit, which after five more millennia came to dominate the crossroads of the four principal trading routes of the time. To the south were Egyptian copper, agricultural products, and a host of luxuries. To the east, along the river routes of the Euphrates and the Tigris, the first domesticated camels brought the agricultural wealth of the Persian Gulf empires as well as treasures from the early cultures of the Indian subcontinent. To the west, olive oil and wine were brought by boat from Cyprus and Greece. And to the north were the kingdoms of Anatolia, where a shrewd bargainer could make deals on iron and copper from the Caucasus and wheat, horses, and human slaves from the steppes of Central Asia. To make your fortune back then, the best advice was to go east – out of Africa and through the Levant, where the wealth of the world awaited.

But it wasn't easy. If fact, it was pretty complicated. Business was conducted at the speed of notches on sticks or, at best, wedge-shaped Cuneiform in wet clay. And though the invention of the Phoenician alphabet helped reduce the complexity of recording transactions, it also brought with it a high overhead cost in hiring the few scribes who could write the new code. In very ancient times, then, the real art – and the hardest part in business – lay in cutting the deals themselves. The essential problem was the method of more efficient exchange, which at the time was limited completely to barter: how many amphorae of wine or olive oil were worth a dozen Lebanese cedars or Scythian stallions? The marketplace needed a better idea to expand beyond the local deal.

The solution was an entirely new idea: money. The man who invented it was Croesus, the king of Lydia, the successor to the ruined Troy of Homer's *Iliad*. Lydia inherited the marvelous riches of the Ionian Greek city-states, especially the silver mines of Pergamum, where modern European tourists now bathe in the altogether amid Greek, Roman, and Turkish ruins. Croesus' idea was elegantly simple: using the electrum, a naturally occurring amalgam of gold and silver, he made coins and guaranteed their standard value. Sardis, his capital, became the world's first banking center. Thus, with one invention Croesus placed his geographi-cally strategic kingdom at the center of the world economy. And, in one of the great comedowns of history, Croesus' money relegated the upper class scribes to bank clerks.

All of our concepts of wealth date from that invention — be they shekels, rubles, dollars, Euros, scratch, bread, dough, sawbucks greenbacks, pesos, doubloons or Federation credits. After Croesus, trade had standards to fall back upon. Price might vary, but *h o w* it varied among different traders became commonly understood. Even today, in recognition of his invention, the truly greedy are still called "rich as Croesus."

The statistics of global wealth – the huge enterprise that trade has become three millennia after Croesus–provides a clearer picture of the world than an atlas. In 1999, the world consumed $24 trillion in goods and services, six times the figure for 1975. Of the world's 6.8 billion people, 4.4 billion live in developing countries, the rest in industrial or transition countries. The three richest people in the world own assets that exceed the combined gross domestic products of the world's poorest 48 countries.

Among the 4.4 billion people who live in developing countries, three-fifths have no access to basic sanitation, almost one-third are without safe drinking water, one-quarter lack adequate housing; one-fifth live beyond the reach of modern health services, one-fifth of the children do not get as far as grade five in school, and one-fifth are undernourished.

The United Nations Human Development Report of 1999 estimates basic education for all would cost $6 billion annually; meanwhile, $8 billion is spent on personal cosmetics in the U.S. alone.

Installation of water and sanitation for all would cost $9 billion, the report estimated, compared with $11 billion spent in Europe each year on ice cream. Reproductive health services for all women would cost $12 billion a year, the same amount spent on perfumes in Europe and the U.S. annually. Basic health care and nutrition would cost $13 billion, $17 billion is spent on pet food each year in Europe and the U.S. More than $35 billion is spent on business and entertainment in Japan, $50 billion on cigarettes in Europe, $105 billion on alcoholic drinks in Europe, $400 billion on narcotic drugs around the world, and $780 billion on the world's militaries.

These UN statistics cannot come close to quantifying the wealth of the world or defining the magnitude of the gap between the "haves" and the "have-nots" of the world. The perspective of the report reflects the UN charter: it shows us the nation-state statistics. But there is, of course, far more to the story. Consider corporate statistics, for example. At present, every one of the Fortune 500 companies is multinational. IBM has a market capitalization of more than $200 billion, larger than the legitimate gross domestic product (GDP) of Colombia. Hewlett Packard is bigger than Greece, Wal-Mart than Argentina, Lucent than South Africa, Qualcomm than Singapore, Cisco than Iran, and Oracle than Chile. More, neither set of statistics gives us insight into the wealth of non-government organizations that are also non-commercial: religious, political, and social organizations all have tremendous wealth in our world today.

For these reasons, we examined the concepts and implications of future *Wealth* carefully in our worlds. We knew, of course, about the have/have-not gap and the rise of the global economy going into our workshops. They are well-documented phenomena here in the year 2000.

But there, in 2020, we wanted to explore the fundamental underpinnings of *Wealth*. It is easy, in our opinion, to wax on about the global economy and the wired world, but it is anyone's guess whether or not those trends will continue. There are many plausible scenarios (and we postulated some) in which they did not.

For us, the questions are not whether a global economy will or will not continue or whether the poor will always be with us. Rather, the central questions were:

- What will people value in the future? For in *Wealth*, there is much *Power* – anciently and in the future.

- How will *Wealth* work in the future? Before Croesus, barter was the method, and goods were independently valuable. After Croesus, money itself filled both roles. We were looking for the possibility of similar revolutions.

- Finally, apart from the physical possession of commodities themselves, how will the *Wealth* of the future be measured in space and time? How will trade, the movement of *Wealth*, be accomplished, measured, and monitored in the future?

At length, we found evidence of broad change afoot. Across all of the scenarios, we saw that money will still be valued in the future. However, in the press of environmental, social, spiritual, and cultural concerns manifested in what we called *Herds*, people increasingly will come to place very high value on less fungible assets, such as knowledge, safety, health, personal networks, and privacy. These new "currencies" and the interrelationships that lead to their acquisition will be more vulnerable to manipulation than money. To some degree, we witnessed the undoing of Croesus' coup: in our futures, things that are valued highly are less easily standardized.

We also saw that significant threats to national well-being will emerge from shifts in the global economy. These threats might result from deliberate "attacks" or they could be spawned by the confluence of myriad economic decisions that are, in turn, based on highly complex interactions and–importantly–transaction flows.

Because opportunities and threats emerge from new or unexpected sources of *Wealth*, it is vital to understand the new forms of economic value creation. In several of our workshops, the participants undertook successful, rudimentary efforts to define models for next-age economic value creation. This effort led us to believe that a more concerted expert-level experiment workshop might bear fruit in the near term.

We also believe that the key to understanding how *Wealth* works in the future lies in building models in which we can define new kinds of observables within dynamic transaction flows. To us, this task is not the same as trying to model how the stock market functions or understanding whether a particular company or sector will increase or decrease in value. Much work is underway on those challenges. Here, we are concerned with what *Wealth* will be and how it will be created and distributed in the future.

Our observations about *Sanctuary* led us to a concern that a significant clash could emerge between that need to monitor *Wealth* and the desire for privacy.

In several of our scenarios, we discovered that a U.S. political policy of isolationism would carry heavy penalties if the rest of the world remained engaged economically. In a global economy, disengagement is difficult. Even the largest world actors cannot walk away from the interconnections of world trade. Thus, U.S. economic policy might outweigh U.S. political policy in a world in which economic decisions have impacts of longer duration. One outgrowth of this observation is that the U.S. Intelligence Community may find itself tasked with monitoring trade and economic treaties.

Finally, as we shall explore in the next chapter, the wellsprings of future *Power* are the values people hold and the things they deem valuable. Therefore, understanding *Wealth* is one of the keys to future national security.

POWER

On February 10, 1519, a Spanish expedition of eleven vessels led by Hernán Cortés rounded the Yucatan Peninsula in search of a wealthy native kingdom rumored to be behind the inland mountains. Cortés was an educated man who had studied law, could read and debate in Latin, and had read the classics that were becoming increasingly available in Europe as the Renaissance wore on. He was also an opportunist; at the age of 19, he left the Old World for the New, where he became a successful planter. Now in his mid-30s, Cortés led 500 soldiers and 100 sailors in hope of fabulous wealth. As a group, they were mixed: bored or failed planters, miners, ex-military men. They were also intensely religious, with an outlook strongly influenced by the crusading spirit of the Middle Ages–it had been in Cortés' own lifetime that the religious wars of Spain ended with the Moors being pushed back from Granada into North Africa.[9] For this generation of Spaniards, Christianity had a military element to it, not unlike a *Jihad*. They believed fervently in the blood of Christ, and they were on a mission to spread that belief.

On the other side of the mountains, it was the year "1 reed" of the fifth era of creation for the Aztec chieftain Montecuhzoma II[10] and his people. The arrival of the Spaniards coincided with the expected return of Quetzalcóatl, the incarnation of a legendary, deified king of the admirable and noble Toltecs, whom the Aztecs had defeated and destroyed centuries before. For the Aztecs, who were among the most frightening people that history records, the arrival of the strangers in Yucatan had the uneasy air of a day of reckoning.

For Aztecs, blood also held religious significance: in creating the fifth era, the gods had used parts of the dead and sprinkled them with fresh blood to create the living. Ritualized war and human sacrifice–ceremonially cutting out the hearts of live hostages with an obsidian blade and throwing them into the temple fire atop the Great Pyramid of their island capital Tenochtitlán–was a central part of the Aztec public life.

When Cortés' soldiers were greeted and escorted peacefully, at first, into the sacred precincts of the capital, they were shocked by the sinister appearance of the Aztec priests.

> They wore black cloaks like cassocks and long gowns reaching to their feet. Some had hoods like those worn by canons, and others had similar hoods like those of the Dominicans, and they wore their hair very long, right down to the waist, and some had it even reaching down to their ankles. Their hair was covered in blood, and so matted together it could not be separated, and their ears were cut to pieces by way of penance. They stank like sulphur and they had another bad smell like carrion. They were the sons of chiefs and abstained from women. They fasted on certain days and what I saw them eat was the pith of seeds. The nails on their fingers were very long, and we heard it said that these priests were very pious and led good lives.[11]

Even to a group not unfamiliar to the acts of the Spanish Inquisition, here was a horror unimagined. These then, were priests who sanctioned crusades of an altogether different sort–called "flower wars" after the beautifully attired warriors who would fall like blossoms– when opposing communities by mutual consent would agree to combat for the sole purpose of capturing prisoners for sacrifice.

The encounter of the Spaniards and the Aztecs is a story often recounted carelessly and rarely examined thoroughly. That is unfortunate. It has many lessons for us today, and– given what we found about the nature of *Power* in our workshops– perhaps more than a few for the future. For that reason, the fall of the Aztecs is worth a brief retelling.

During their march inland toward Tenochtitlán, the Spaniards encountered and formed an alliance with a native tribe, the Tlaxcalans, whom the Aztecs had alienated. Montecuhzoma, fearing the religious implications of the landing party, greeted them with cautious, but open arms. The Europeans were welcomed across the causeways of Lake Texcoco to the capital city, where more than 300,000 people lived and worked on an island in the middle. Once there, in a city larger than their Cordoba or Seville, the Spaniards found themselves effectively hostages, trapped in an island city of warriors.

After about two weeks, Cortés and his men set upon an incredibly bold plan. Asking for an audience with the Aztec chief on a pretext, they seized the shocked Montecuhzoma inside the royal apartments. For the Aztecs this move was more than surprising, it was unimaginable. The king was not only an unquestioned religious figure, his very personage was sacred. Dazed and bewildered, Montecuhzoma allowed himself to be escorted across the central plaza of the city under the amazed eyes of his subjects. Despite the chieftain's public claims that he accompanied the Spaniards willingly, from then onward, Montecuhzoma had lost the initiative and was never to regain it. In one bold move, the Spaniards had succeeded in holding thousands of warriors at bay by playing on the Aztec belief in the invincibility of their leader.

After that, Cortés' demands of the captive were endless. Members of his party were allowed to visit the Aztec gold mines. Sacred sites outside of the city were explored. Montecuhzoma was forced to declare his vassalage to Charles V of Spain. The final demand, the spark that set the Aztec world aflame, was the placement of a Christian place of worship atop the Great Pyramid. In full view of the city, the Spanish worshipers now set about to ascend the steps with a crucifix and an image of the Virgin. The Indian nobles and priests were enraged and exploded into open revolt. When Montecuhzoma was made by the Spaniards to stand on the rooftop of the pyramid to calm his people, he was greeted first with incredulous silence, and then with whistles and jeers, and finally with stones and arrows until he fell with concussion and died of his wounds.

Cortés' men then stormed the pyramid, and atop the very summit of the most sacred of Aztec places, the Spaniards and the Aztec warriors fought each other with no quarter in full view of the city. In the end, Cortés prevailed, casting down the Aztec idols into the streets below and setting fire to the chambers of the Great Pyramid until a gigantic smoke plume arose from the city for all the horrified countryside to see. The Spaniards fought their way to escape across the lake, only to return three months later for a full and successful siege. Montecuhzoma's successor was hanged, and almost all of the Aztec nobility—men, women, and children—were put to the sword. A great cathedral was erected atop the Great Pyramid, and the religious practices, political power, and culture of the Aztecs were forever extinguished.

In our five *Protean* worlds, to our surprise, we found that *Power* had more in common with this gruesome and complicated story from 500 years ago than the experience of the past 70 years. For much of the 20th century, Western ideas of power and threat have been focused on specific nation-state actors. Nazi Germany and Imperial Japan preoccupied Allied foreign policy from the 1930s to the end of World War II, with little more than a pause and a shift in focus to the Soviet empire.

In our workshops, however, we found very little linkage with the military-political model of *Power* in the future. In *Amazon.plague*, it stemmed from health and health care. In *Militant Shangri-La*, it arose from the ability to create a huge banking empire and an influential, global media network. In *Yankee Going Home*, voter unwillingness to support foreign policy essentially imposed an isolationist policy on Congress, sharply limiting U.S. power and influence in a global economy. In *The Enemy Within*, *Power* was vested in factionalism. In *New Camelot*, it meant high-technology industry and global enterprise.

The underpinnings of *Power* were not inherent in the scenarios; we did not build them into story line. Rather, in living and working in these futures, our participants were faced with the dilemma of understanding where and how threats to national security arose. To get to that point, they found in every case that they had to collectively explore the nature of *Power* in their worlds. Who had it?

How did they get it? What were its vulnerabilities? How could those vulnerabilities be exploited by a future Intelligence Community?

In every case, the nature and/or distribution of *Power* changed in significant ways from what we see today, not because the geopolitical construct of the worlds was different, but because — in one way or another – *Power always hinged on values.* In other words, when values change in the world, even at the grass roots, the *Power* structure of the world also changes.

No doubt, this will perhaps be less a revelation to some readers than it was for us, living as we do in the workaday world of government. For us, however, it meant that there was some complex correlation among changing values in the world, a resulting change in *Power,* and ultimately the creation of opportunities and threats. That kind of equation does not reduce well to a set of office codes or military commands, and even less to the ideas conveyed in *Joint Vision 2010* or the *Quadrennial Defense Review.* Objectives like "battle space dominance" and the generic ability to fight multiple wars in multiple parts of the world simultaneously fail to capture the richness of the insight we had that, in the long run, threat depends less on what people *have* than on what people *think.*

We think, therefore, that *Power* is a concept, which in its broadest strategic context requires much exploration by the Intelligence Community and its partners in government. We are not suggesting that it will be easy to do. We understand that it is much easier to think about and to react to *Power* when you think of it as relatively static and concrete entities – tank barrels, ICBM silos, or anthrax ampoules–that can be counted and measured. Our findings about future *Power* were much like our findings about future *Wealth* – it's the flow that matters in strategic issues. That, we agree, unrepentantly, is very hard. Our concern is that intelligence professionals not be satisfied with the easier analysis because we saw in our worlds that it is very dangerous to do so.

In a world of changing values, *Power* is temporal. The idea of "great powers" then – like the idea of "spheres of influence" from our chapter on *Starlight* – is for us a Victorian concept that has almost no relevance in worlds in which empowerment has so many diverse origins.

Our experience taught us clearly that if you do not understand or lack insight into either existing or emerging values, then you will not be able to understand the full dimensionality of the *Power* abroad in your world. Two corollaries follow:

- Lacking such insight, instruments of *Power* accumulated over time—political, economic, cultural, religious, military—inevitably will erode and perhaps become irrelevant. When *Power* erodes or it is an inappropriate match to an adversary, the best case is a sort of strategic impotence. The worst case is that you are open to strategic surprise.

- Failure to understand the full dimensionality of *Power* risks blindness to instruments of power that can threaten you.

Moreover, what *Power* is today and what it will be tomorrow will depend on the extent to which values are shared – or at least understood. Viewed from the hindsight of our 2020 worlds, the most dangerous moments in history are those when *Herds* are on the move. In such moments, the possibility for misunderstanding is high, the instruments of *Power* are changing, the strong are confident in their strength, and the weak are considering new strategies.

The special case represented by the Aztec-Conquistador conflagration is especially disconcerting. When dissimilar entities with different values meet, the dissimilarities are in multiple dimensions (cultural, political, military, religious) and the stakes are high, the collision is invariably violent and reaction time is short. To see and characterize the resulting conflict in only one dimension is to miss the deeper underpinnings of the dispute and, in consequence, much of the potential for resolving it. In this context we found it valuable within our workshops to take the conflict apart in all its dimensions to determine if it was just very *complicated* or whether it was genuinely *complex*. The conflict today in Sierra Leone fits the former model in our view: its causes, if not its consequences, are relatively straightforward. The conflict in Zaire, the wars in the Middle East, and the disintegration of Indonesia in 1999 are much more complex problems because they stem from dissimilarities in multiple dimensions.

Finally, our work gave us a specific insight into the nature of instruments of *Power*. In a nutshell, technology matters – a lot. For the Spaniards, cannon, crossbows, metal helmets, and horses proved to be decisive once the conflict had begun. If they fought well and chose their ground, technology proved, indeed, to be a force multiplier. In our future worlds, we found the same linkage. No matter what challenge was presented, our workshop participants proved themselves to be consummate technologists who had as much mastery over their milieu as a Spanish swordsman over Castilian steel. Cognizant as we are that our *Insights* bring many worries and much uncertainty, we hasten to bring that as good news as well.

No subject received more visibility in our workshops than the Internet.[12] It was clear from the outset that this remarkable new venue for human enterprise was dominating almost everyone's thinking. This realization was particularly true for the intelligence professionals who were skilled in signals intelligence (SIGINT). For many of these very accomplished and specialized technologists, there was a belief that most of the intelligence problems of the future could somehow be mitigated if only we could chart the Internet with very fine detail. Their approach was much like that of submariners, for whom a detailed chart of the ocean bottom landscape was an invaluable tool in underwater warfare. For the SIGINT specialists, there was a similar and almost irresistible urge to dive into the topology of the Internet. For the workshop facilitators, however, the challenge was very different: it was to keep the technologists from diving deep into server routings and metadata long enough to examine some alternative possibilities. In the end, the two groups arrived at a set of metaphors that, taken together, provide a much deeper understanding. We begin with the first: the Internet as a *Parallel Universe*.

In the ten years since the Internet has gone mainstream, spreading the Information Revolution at light speed across the globe, no topic has gained more interest, debate – and funding – in the Intelligence Community than Information Warfare. In 1993, the NSA literally reinvented itself around the problem. Two years later, as hacking attempts splashed increasingly across the public media, the FBI launched a campaign to build a large-scale counter-cyberterrorism capability. Each of the military Services have also made significant expenditures and built information-enabled combat doctrines.

Simply put, Information Warfare has become one of the few growth areas in government and is probably the fastest-growing government national security investment since the rise of the space program in the late 1960s. Inside many government agencies and departments, the emerging Information Warfare mission resembles the Oklahoma Land Rush—everyone is racing for a place in line.

Spurring the rush on, the rise of the so-called "New Economy," based on information-enabled inventory management and first-to-market intelligence, was touted by some military theorists as the harbinger of revolutionary kinds of warfare. In particular, the Navy has formulated Network-Centric Warfare around parallel business concepts it calls "self-synchronizing forces" and "speed of command." Then, at the close of the last decade, the rise of the "dot com" companies reflected an increasing manifestation of the Internet as a definable, if virtual, destination.

Finally, it became apparent on New Year's Day 2000 that the global rush to combat Y2K not only worked, but it had also resulted in massive upgrading of software worldwide. Some estimate that the price tag for this upgrade was $500 billion, with the result that the mercantile infrastructure of the world and the workplace for most of the world's knowledge workers is now in superb shape.

Now that the terrestrial infrastructure is maturing, and no less than five satellite constellations for global Internet access may be on the launch pad in the next two years, content is becoming king –as the Wall Street buzz phrase goes. We all seem poised for a massive uploading of a huge new global knowledge base. We might be better off thinking of the post-Cold War period as the post-Gutenberg Age.

The world has changed, and few doubt the change is near complete. There are, therefore, fewer targets more challenging and worrisome than the future global Internet, where *Wealth* and *Power* will flow along silicon gates, tempting the world's opportunists. But is the Intelligence Community thinking about the Internet in the right way? Is the huge amount of resources–time, money, and manpower – being invested in exploitation strategies that will pay off?

One of the key insights we gained in *Proteus* was a worrisome answer to that question: maybe not. Today, most of the effort to understand Information Warfare is based on analogies of cryptology, which was radio-circuit based. In 20th century cryptology, most of the intelligence insights were gained not from breaking the codes, but in two other technical approaches: observing the pathways and identifying the nodes of the traffic. The first technique, called "traffic analysis," sought to build a map of the radio nets by charting one of several possible "external" variables (that is, categorization and routing information tacked on to the message as a preamble, and often unencrypted, rather than the message content itself). The second method was to carefully capture and examine the analog (later digital) signatures of modems and multiplexing schemes of the transmissions. Meticulously cataloging this technical data gave cryptologists insight into what kinds of information might be contained within the message, if not the plain text itself.

In the Intelligence Community today, most attempts to understand and exploit the Internet are the intellectual progeny of those radio-circuit techniques. Massive efforts are underway to catalog the growing topology of the global communications infrastructure with the idea that, like surreptitious toll takers, cryptologists can somehow take notes as the digits go whizzing by. With its long history of successful radio-network exploitation and deep technical expertise, the Intelligence Community tends to see the future of the Internet as an extrapolation of the past – an evolutionary development of the previous communication target. Billions of dollars are in the programmatic queue to view the future Internet along these lines.

At first glance, this metaphor makes good sense. This approach to cryptology worked well in the past, and the Internet *is* technical, after all. A closer examination, however, raises the question: is the radio-circuit model the right metaphor for thinking about the technical nature of the future Internet? If it is, then our billions are being well spent. If it isn't, then we may be squandering scarce post-Cold War defense resources and risking blindness by limiting our imaginations to a kind of virtual world that will not come to be.

At length, in our discussions, we concluded that this view of the Internet is dangerously limiting. To capture a larger set of possibilities, we began to think of the Internet as an emerging and fundamentally new kind of *destination* – a universe parallel to the physical one. In this metaphor, the Internet that we see today is akin to the Earth in Cambrian times, when biological life underwent an unprecedented explosion of speciation. New life cropped up everywhere—more than 300,000 new distinct forms in a geologic instant.

If the Internet is a *Parallel Universe*–a silicon-based version of the carbon-based one we know—then the incredible uploading of global knowledge we are about to experience might produce a digital Cambrian explosion in which an amazing array of digital "beings" will arise. And, if that is true, then present attempts to understand the future Internet topographically will be like trying to understand the development of life on Earth by meticulously cataloging its geology!

Bad news, that. Biology isn't geology. Sentient beings arise in complex ways, whereas inert matter responds to a more Newtonian rhythm. If we do experience a "Digital Cambrian," then the rise and interactions of complex software will be understandable only in terms of chaos mathematics, about which we have only an adolescent appreciation in the early 2000s. In a Digital Cambrian, all kinds of unpredictable digital life could emerge—from software herbivores that graze the knowledge bases of tomorrow to frightening new kinds of predators that would make today's hackers look like little salamanders. Most frightening, these digital beings leave only virtual trails—we can imagine them, but we can't actually see them. If we only imagine the *geology* of the future Internet, we won't see the *biology* that others—perhaps an adversary—might. It takes little imagination to figure out where that asymmetry might lead.

Thinking of the Internet as a *Parallel Universe* helped us significantly because it conveyed the sense of a destination. We found this much more useful than thinking of it as network, however sophisticated. But even that conception inadequately captured the enormous role the Internet played in our futures. Across every world–even we tried to invent scenarios that minimized its relevance–cyberspace became a key enabler of human activity and an underpinning of the world order. Virtual enterprises and activities ranging from global schools to electronic religion flowed along a future Internet that came to be seen as a definer of community and a theater for welfare, competition, and subversion.

A second metaphor, the internet as a theater, became as useful to us as the *Parallel Universe* model. In at least two of the worlds, *The Enemy Within* and *Militant Shangri-La*, the Internet allowed vast illusions and great deceptions to be played out while the authors remained hidden in the shadows. The Internet is a near-perfect venue for perception management on a global scale. As we observed in the chapters on *Veracity*, *Wealth*, and *Herds*, ideas move around the globe so fast in a wired world that it is difficult to pull them back once they are set in motion. At the same time, the ideas of distinctly offensive and defensive actions become distorted.

Indeed, the tempo of the future Internet became cause for great concern on our part. Neither the metaphors of *Parallel Universe* nor a world theater captured the temporal nature of the Internet well. In the end, we came to appreciate that the Internet was a place where time–not space–was the defining dimension. To perceive the Internet properly, we must find ways to build a cognitive interface that will allow analysts–who, after years of biological evolution possess marvelous senses for spatial considerations – to live in a world driven increasingly by time. To say it in an even more mind-boggling way, we think the future Internet is a place where sophisticated software agents evolve and interact in complex ways in time, not space. It is an alien planet with very different life forms in a different dimension. But actions and events carried out on that "planet" have complex and near immediate effects on the world in which humans live.

As if all that weren't enough, we found yet another important aspect to the Internet that required yet another metaphor. Because it is both the reservoir for the world's knowledge as well as a conduit for trade and commerce, access to the Internet literally determines the boundary between "haves" and "have-nots." In educational circles, this realization is captured in the term "digital divide," meaning that students who have access to the Internet have more information and better learning resources than those who do not. This concept is also true about economics in the future. Thus, the Internet is like a river: where it flows, "haves" will arise. Where it does not, "have-nots" will arise. We saw some very practical analytical consequences of this observation: by monitoring the growth (and delays in growth) in the global communications infrastructure, it may be possible to gain insight into the nature, growth, and distribution of global *Wealth*.

Given our observations that *Wealth* and *Power* are interrelated with values and that the Internet is a powerful theater for perception management, understanding where the river flows at any given time may be very important indeed. To that end, it is worth reiterating the point that new ways of mapping and modeling the world may be much more central to the Intelligence Community's future mission than the mere act of sensing it.

Despite the complexity of our comparisons and the significant challenges that they convey, we came away from our deliberations with mixed news for intelligence practitioners. On the one hand, the Internet is a great leveler: it takes little specialized knowledge and few resources for a hostile entity to use it in a plethora of ways to threaten the U.S., and some of those options are both subtle and insidious. On the other hand, at least within the community of nation states, nowhere on the planet is more research ongoing on the future Internet than in the U.S. The challenge is to avoid oversimplification: life is not a bowl of cherries, and the Internet is not a network.

For nearly all the *Proteus* participants the construct of the Intelligence Community itself—its organization and makeup—was a preoccupation. In the opening sessions in early 1999, the idea of the Intelligence Community was almost always conveyed as an organizational chart with the various three-letter agencies wired together by mission relationships. This idea was a very natural approach, not unlike one would find in any other sector of professional life. Put airline executives in a conference room, and they will quickly draw the airline industry in the same way: rectangles attached by lines.

Recognizing this propensity, one of the goals of the NRO sponsor from the outset was unusual. The NRO wanted to delve into the future problem space at large, leaving aside the existing set of organizational relationships in order to better understand what *ought* to be built to cope with the worlds we explored. This approach is most unusual, and in the opinion of the Deloitte facilitators, it was this willingness not just to think "outside the box", but to erase it altogether that led to the richness of the *Insights* we gained as a team.

Our final insight, *Bedfellows*, requires little further analogy than the name implies. Throughout the process, it became obvious to everyone involved that the people the Intelligence Community will need in the future would be different than those who are in the component organizations now.

At the center of our experience was that global complexity accelerated in all the worlds, even when–as in *Yankee Going Home*–the U.S. tried to disengage. At the same time, the economic component of national security increased as the world economy and information infrastructures grew and tended to upstage military, diplomatic, and political components. This meant that, in every case, national security changed – as did the logically derived intelligence functions, priorities, and players. In short, there were more players, *and* what the IC needed to know was different. In the next phase of our investigation, *Proteus II*, we will conduct another workshop with three central questions in mind:

- What kinds of information would a future U.S. Intelligence Community need to deal with the challenges in each world?

- Where is that information likely to be found?

- How would the Community obtain it?

In careful examination of these questions in the workshop, and in subsequent games in other *Proteus* efforts, we will seek to build a list of specific skill sets the Community will likely need in the future. Thus, *Bedfellows* is an enduring topic. Here, it is enough to detail seven observations from the initial workshops.

First, if we had not held both "insider" and "outsider" workshops, much would have been missed. The different perspectives of the two groups were sometimes stunning. For example, when we worked in the *New Camelot* world, which was intended by the authors to be a largely peaceful world, the outsiders were content to experience it that way. The intelligence professionals, however, found significant threats and challenges that were completely over-looked by the outsiders. The same was true of *Militant Shangri-la*, a very complex scenario deliberately written to be interpreted in the eye of the beholder. For the outsiders, a threat was present, but it was a subject of considerable debate. For the insiders, the threat was immediate and obvious.

Our first reaction in our *in camera* discussions of the workshop outcomes was to label the insiders as cynics who found threats behind every tree. More reflection, however, showed that to be a hasty conclusion: the threats they found were real, significant, and profoundly changed our idea of what threat is. Gradually, some of us came to see the outsiders as naïve. In the end, we confess, we are still in an internal debate: and therein lies the value of con-stantly attracting new people into the Community.

Second, to be effective in our worlds the Intelligence Community needed both new partners and new customers – almost continu-ally. As a result, the idea of the Community as a static entity – an organizational chart with well-defined participants, roles, and mis-sions – emerged as an anachronism.

Third, rapidly changing demands and the dynamism of the sce-narios repeatedly placed a premium on organizational agility–con-tingency planning, virtual organizations, and other flexible ap-proaches–perhaps over technology investment. In other words, the *Starlight* problem required the intelligence professionals to see emerging patterns and begin to react to them organizationally be-fore the entire sequence of events unfolded. Because threats to national security arose from economic, political, social, biologi-cal, and other situations, the Community nearly always had to have

–in place–broadly experienced reaction teams to be effective. This concept was particularly true when the sequence of events was genuinely complex and not merely complicated.

Fourth, we saw opportunities where efficiencies and additional resources could be gained by outsourcing non-critical intelligence needs and building partnerships across intelligence and non-intelligence agencies, corporations, and NGOs.

Fifth, because partners, customers, and the Intelligence Community itself all changed internally at different rates and in response to different (and sometimes even the same) stimuli, it may be necessary in the future to expand the current concept of firewalls and tripwires to establish real-time or predictive indications and warnings of situational changes among them. To be effective, intelligence leaders had to understand not only the enemies, but also the allies – all of whom were experiencing high rates of change.

Sixth, because today's friend might be tomorrow's foe, the Community had to recognize that unpredictable and shifting alignments of partners and competitors brought significant complexity to role and mission definitions.

Finally, and to close again on a hopeful note, we found that the expertise, data, and analysis that the Intelligence Community needed almost always was available–if it looked outside itself. Indeed, there were instances–notably in biological warfare–where a relatively small coordination effort on the part of the Community could yield very large returns today.

One of the surprise books of the millennium year was Irish Poet Laureate Seamus Heaney's new translation of the great 10th century epic poem, *Beowulf*.[13] Long has it been the bane of high school sophomores in the English-speaking world! Until Heaney—whose abandonment of academic English for a guttural Irish translation infuses the battle between Beowulf and the marauding dragon Grendel with remarkable energy and, above all, action:

> Now the weapon was to prove its worth.
> The warrior determined to take revenge
> for every gross act Grendel had committed—
> ...Beowulf in his fury
> now settled the score: he saw the monster
> in his resting place, war-weary and wrecked,
> a lifeless corpse, a casualty
> of the battle of Heorot. The body gaped
> at the stroke dealt to it after death:
> Beowulf cut the corpse's head off.[14]

You can almost see Arnold Swartzennegger in the leading role. To the delight of literature teachers everywhere, Heaney's *Beowulf* rose to the top of the bestseller lists and stayed there for weeks.

Unless you are looking for lessons on dragon slaying, much of the power and the message in the epic lies in the fact that the men and women of *Beowulf* exist simultaneously in two worlds. Their hearts and minds are infused with ancient, inherited pagan traditions, but there is also the emerging Celtic Christianity that has managed to gain a foothold in their souls, pulling and tugging them both. They can neither quite let go of the one, nor fully embrace the other.

> Sometimes at pagan shrines they vowed
> Offerings to the idols, swore oaths
> That the killer of souls might come to their aid
> And save the people. That was their way,
> Their heathenish hope; deep in their hearts
> They remembered hell.[15]

Old ways, old instincts die hard. Heaney's translation makes the struggle between the last Dragon and the last Warrior the monumental event that it is: the imminent passing of an age. Because it does, it is timely reading for all of us. Willingly or not, we must all go into the future, whatever it portends.

What next, then? For *Proteus*, these *Insights* are not enough, clearly. It is not enough to point to problems. This document, therefore, can only be an intermezzo before a greater effort that moves us toward solutions. We need real strategies to meet the challenges of the futures we have found. More, we need methodologies to examine those strategies dynamically in light of persistent programmatic and operational rhythms of government. And, it is clear that there will be specific technology families in the future that will be key to executing those strategies. These three issues define the scope of work for the *Proteus* project in the next six months.

Proteus II involves additional workshops with the specific aim of taking subject matter experts through a set of questions that lead to the construction of notional intelligence systems. We will ask them what kinds of information they need to resolve specific intelligence problems in their worlds, where that information can be found, and how they might obtain it. We'll want to know what kinds of systems will be needed in the future to get that information, to analyze it, and to deliver it to customers. And, we'll want to know what kinds of technologies are key to those systems. Finally, we will take the notional systems and technologies into a specially constructed sixth scenario—*The Lexus Hit the Olive Tree*—where we will stress test our findings and recommend strategies for the NRO.

In *Proteus III*, we will engage some of the best mathematical talent in the world to develop a new kind of gaming environment, in which both complicated and complex phenomenon can be examined. From that we intend to initiate a recurring cycle of games to help the Intelligence Community examine its existing, planned, and postulated systems.

In *Proteus IV*, we are building a capability within the NRO to scrutinize specific emerging technologies and scientific techniques. Our goal is to master these technologies, which we perceive to be the key to sustaining the edge over adversaries, present and future. We want to understand the critical paths for technology convergence, the market forces that shape technology development, and where and when to provide funds for those key technologies that are not developing in the commercial world.

In the end, the *Insights* gained from the *Proteus* worlds left us with a mixed picture of the future. That may be the proof that we are onto something: whatever else the future portends, it surely will be mixed. There are confusing glimpses, for example, such as *Veracity*, in which the concept of bedrock truth is shaken. And *Small Stuff* and *Parallel Universe* both raise the even more stunning prospect that our very ideas of life might expand greatly in the future.

Yet, throughout our effort we were able to see three strengths in our groups which lead us to believe that the Intelligence Community can, indeed, go successfully into the future—whatever it portends.

Foremost among them was the remarkable willingness at all levels of the NRO not merely to observe change, but to jump in with both feet, searching for problems and solutions alike. Indeed, one of the great challenges for the facilitators was to hold some the participants back until the whole group acclimated to the world! Any notion that the NRO is hidebound in the Cold War was dispelled in the *Proteus* effort: here is an organization that is both vibrant and far-seeing.

Second, our observations from *Bedfellows* about the need to continually refresh the gene pool in Intelligence notwithstanding, the incredible talent brought to bear in the hundreds of people who participated in *Proteus* has been encouraging in itself. No matter what kind of problem a scenario presented—from law enforcement and sociology to nanotechnology and economics to more traditional military and diplomatic support—expertise was almost immediately within our grasp. Few countries—let alone government agencies—can command the kind of intellectual capital that we witnessed.

Finally, beyond talent, there was also vast experience, which is a different sort of commodity. Gradually across our deliberations, it became obvious to us that–apart from the NRO–the number of organizations on the planet that have a long and successful history of devising, executing, and maintaining very large, high-technology enterprises are few and far between. In the U.S., those that do are almost all associated with the aerospace industry and, more often than not, they are partners of the NRO. Thus, like shipyards that can build aircraft carriers and submarines, we came to understand the NRO is a key part of the industrial base of the country.

In all of our *Protean* futures, even a highly theoretical Intelligence Community needed an organization like the NRO. In *Amazon.plague*, for example, no amount of medical expertise or multinational cooperation was sufficient to resolve the central dilemma of where the virus would strike next. That took a very different skill set than that of doctors and professional politicians. The same proved true in *Militant Shangri-la*, where economic transaction flows were one of the key threats to Western security. While we had a number of experienced economists participating in the workshops, their contribution generally helped only to understand what wealth was in the world. It took a different mentality to chart the transaction flows, find the observables, and identify critical points for action.

Thus, after 18 months of effort, we left the first phase of *Proteus* with a sense of unease about the future, but also great confidence in the Intelligence Community and its people. In our search for weakness in the Community, we also found strength. In the end, we also found that no amount of cynicism could dispel the central truth that the U.S. Intelligence Community provided the nation the information it needed to escape the horrendous evils of the latter half of the 20ᵗʰ century, and to prevail. We are confident that it will do so in the future, as well. As Heaney puts it better than we can:

> And now this is 'an inheritance'—
> Upright... unshiftably planked
> In the long ago, yet willingly forward
> Again and again and again.[16]

SCENARIO-BASED PLANNING FOR TECHNOLOGY INVESTMENTS

By Charles W. Thomas

Technology decisions are among the most crucial that a company makes. Investing in unique high-technology offerings or service capabilities to gain competitive advantage is a strategic decision best made with top management's full participation and understanding.

Good technology choices are those that have the potential to succeed in a variety of possible future markets. Bad choices gamble a company's competitive position on the arrival of only one possible future. If that "single-point forecast" does not emerge, the stage is set for a slide into noncompetitiveness. Scenario planning can help management make better technology decisions by better understanding the choices—both the opportunities and the risks involved in preparing for a dynamic, turbulent, and uncertain future market.

A team of technical experts that evaluates a technology in terms of its uniqueness, performance growth potential, or against the current competition is likely to miss critical future marketing opportunities and fail to see important potential risks, especially nontraditional ones. Though developers have detailed knowledge of an emerging technology or have developed a superior product, market success is not guaranteed. In contrast, when scenario-based technology planning is skillfully employed, it combines a thorough knowledge of the technology with a wide-ranging assessment of what the future market will demand. Scenarios can help managers evaluate the technology future customers will need.

The second section of this chapter will be devoted to various applications of scenarios to technology decisions, as demonstrated in four case studies. But before looking at applications, we must set some ground rules about scenario planning and how technology scenarios are developed. Scenarios are decision-making tools, and like all good tools, scenarios must be used correctly, and for the appropriate job.

DEVELOPING SCENARIOS FOR TECHNOLOGY DECISION MAKING

Scenarios are developed first by casting your net widely to identify the many potential issues, trends, and factors in the business environment—past, present, and future—that can have an impact on your business. These issues and trends are called *business drivers*, and whether your objective is to explore the corporate business portfolio strategy or a technology investment strategy, you should not restrict this initial research and brainstorming activity. No matter how narrow your planning objectives, it is crucial to consider all influences at this early stage.

Don't fall into the trap of seeking out "good" drivers and ignoring "bad" ones. In the context of future business environments, you will not know which are important drivers and which can be ignored, so collect all the potential significant influences. These can be systemwide issues, such as global war or the power of the World Trade Organization; and issues closer to home, for instance, worker education programs or your corporate benefits package. Drivers can be issues over which you have influence (regulatory legislation or the level of your technology investment) or those you do not (the U.S. national debt or the liquidity of unfunded pension liabilities in France).

When you have compiled a broad list of significant influences, the next step is to reduce the breadth of your examination and bring some rigor and systematic analysis to categorizing the business drivers. This step involves clustering and synthesizing all the drivers (typically as many as 150 to 200) into the macrolevel issues that define the overall decision-planning environment. There macrolevel clusters become the fundamental assumptions of your planning effort, the base assumptions upon which you build the scenarios. These macrolevel assumptions are called *dimensions*. They define the boundaries (dimensions) of the scenario planning space. Where drivers have no rules of inclusion and exclusion, dimensions have very specific rules:

- They are defined at a macrolevel.

- Their future "state" is uncertain.

- They are factors over which your organization has no control.

To understand this process better, try imaging the visual image of a cube in "future space." Somewhere inside that cube is where your company's future lies. The dimensions of the cube define your planning space. The first task is to make sure that the cube encompasses all the issues relevant to your business. Everything you, your colleagues, and external experts think is important to consider must be "inside" that cube—those are the business drivers. When you define the dimensions, you are describing the boundaries of that cube or planning space. By defining the dimensions, you are setting the boundary conditions of the planning environment. Eventually, you will be choosing your planning scenarios from the inside of that cube.

A Defense Contractor Example

The management team of a typical scenario-planning effort will nominate between 125 and 200 businesses drivers. For example, the drivers nominated by a defense contractor planning team might include: global defense alliances; economic competitiveness; ethnic tensions in Europe; types of weaponry available; Japanese economic policies; state and local business and tax incentives; types of warfare; U.S. economic strength; global free trade; number of graduates in engineering disciplines; terrorism; sources of conflict; the globalization of industry; isolationist foreign policy; location of conflicts; frequency of conflicts; telecommunications developments.

The dimensions selected to define the planning environment emerge from a clustering of the business drivers. For example, clustering some of the drivers just given (types of warfare, location of conflicts, terrorism, sources of conflict, and frequency of conflicts) suggests that one possible dimension is Level of Global Political Instability. Sometimes a driver becomes a dimension (the strength of the U.S. economy, for example) but that is rare. More frequently, managers select appropriate dimensions after they categorize, synthesize, merge, and blend the large set of original business drivers into macrolevel dimensions. The goal is to select those dimensions that will represent future market and business issues in ways that stretch conventional wisdom and encourage innovative thinking, yet still present the business environment in ways that are meaningful to the operating managers.

Selecting the dimensions is difficult work and involves about half science and half art. It also requires good teamwork between the scenario team and line managers. In this defense contractor case, the company managers began with about 175 business drivers nominated from research, internal and external interviews, and a final "brainstorming meeting" intended to explore the interrelationships among the drivers. Such a meeting is often a great help in clustering the drivers into macrolevel dimensions. In this case, the clustering and analysis of drivers produced four dimensions that were used to set the boundary conditions and define the variations in the future business environment in a way meaningful to the company's strategic business interests:

- The level of U.S. global involvement;

- The level of global instability;

- Countervailing military power (to the United States);

- U.S. economic vitality.

The dimensions were then arrayed in a matrix to produce a "scenario space" from which the scenarios were to be selected. The next task was to select the minimum number of scenarios from that planning space that together captured the range of threats and opportunities that must be explored (see Exhibit 1). The scenarios were chosen to reflect the need for a defense firm to think about the range of its business opportunities and constraints, and the products and technologies it should develop to accommodate a range of future business settings.

This defense firm project, circa 1988, was primarily an effort to make some critical long-term strategic decisions about technology investment. Yet, despite its importance to the study, technology was not among the defining dimensions of the planning space. Usually, technology makes a poor defining dimension (or assumption) for scenarios intended to be used for technology decisions. That is often a hard predisposition to overcome. Technology-based firms are comfortable with technology concepts, and, after all, they wish to make technology decisions. But using technology terms to define the planning setting—the scenarios— can cause serious problems.

The decisions faced by the defense contractor illustrate this problem. The first dilemma was, How do we define a technology dimension? What macrolevel expression can be used to capture future technology states?

Initially, the managers thought of defining some worlds as "high technology" and some as "low technology." Later, and perhaps more realistically, they tried "high technology growth" and "low technology growth." But as they thought through the implications of those dimensions, they asked themselves, "Why should we expect that all the technologies will develop in similar ways or at similar pace?" And, "Isn't the potential for differential growth in competing technologies something we might want to test?" Finding a satisfactory technology dimension that does not restrict your planning options turns out to be quite difficult.

A serious planning (and logic) dilemma is produced when the very thing you want to explore—potential technology investments—is fixed as a defining assumption of the planning environment. Finally, the defense contractor's managers concluded that, for them, technology

Exhibit 1
Scenario Space: Future Global Defense Market to 2005-2010¹

	Name²	Level of U.S. Global Involvement³		Countervailing Military Power²		U.S. Economic Vitality		Level of Gobal Involvement	
		High	Low	Focused	Diffuse	Vibrant	Weak	High	Low
1	U.S. Driven Market								
2									
3	Dangerous Property								
4									
5	Regional Markets								
6	Peace and Prosperity								
7	Confused Priorities								
8									
9									
10									
11									
12									
13									
14	Isolationist Dream								
15									
16									

¹Average weapon system R&D cycles in the defense industries are between 10 and 15 years. This planning horizon was chosen to take the analysis beyond consideration of products currently "in the pipeline".
²Named worlds are those chosen for analysis. They are selected to represent the plausible range of opportunities and constraints to be faced.
³Included military, economic, and diplomatic involvement.
⁴Is military power in the world "focused" on counteracting the "American preponderance", or is it more generally aimed at various local and regional threats.

was too important an unknown to make possibly unwarranted assumptions about at the beginning of the planning effort.

Technology is often one of a firm's most promising ways to respond to or to create a future business environment. The planners who develop the scenarios should select strong and robust technologies suitable in a range of futures. The scenarios should not constrain their imaginations about technology.

Scenarios provide managers with plausible hypothetical business environments where they can test and explore the viability of a range of technologies. But how can scenarios depict opportunities in technology investments if technology is not part of the definition of the future world they describe? First, the scenarios must provide rich detail about the forces that drive personal and business decisions so that the scenario user can decide which technologies will flourish. For example, the scenarios should provide detail about the business and lifestyle priorities of your customers, and where appropriate, of your customers' customers. Well-drawn scenarios simulate complex, richly detailed, often confusing business environments into which managers can venture armed with their business expertise and ask, "Which products and technologies would work here?"

However, scenarios that are intended to aid in long-term technology investment decisions have some special requirements. The planning horizon must extend well beyond the current R&D cycle to divorce future technology decisions from the biases caused by technologies currently in the pipeline. The scenario environments must contain certain information required for technology decision-making.

Although information needs differ from industry to industry, there are some common threads. The terms at which capital resources will be available—the cost of investment capital, the status of interest rates and inflation, government monetary and fiscal policies—must be addressed in each scenario. Trends in regulatory issues—not just those directly affecting the technology but background regulations like those of the Environmental Protection Agency (EPA) or Office of Safety and Health Administration (OSHA)—also must be well documented. If the time horizon is a bit distant, attention should be paid to trends in technical graduate schools and changes in the general social setting for the introduction of new technologies.

The scenario team should not be content merely to enumerate the list of technology decision drivers and include them in the scenarios. The scenarios must provide the logic for thorough analysis of those drivers and their interrelationships. For example, not only must capital availability be examined in all three scenarios:

- Available but very expensive;

- Tightly controlled by government priorities;

- All but nonexistent in the advanced industrial countries but flowing in the emerging markets.

In addition, the interrelationship between capital and other key drivers must be logically explored. This process is critical if the scenarios are to be a reasonable reflection of true business issues.

Finally, scenarios should be used to challenge an organization's conventional wisdom. Scenarios offer an opportunity to test the assumptions that a firm simply never thinks to question, such as, "The infrastructure investments needed to enter our industry are so huge that we have an effective barrier to new competitors."

Assume that you have developed a set of scenarios for your specific organizational planning needs. The scenarios capture the range of threats and opportunities for which you must plan, and they thoroughly assess both the business environment and the priorities of your customers. In addition, assume that the scenarios were developed initially for corporate planning and that the firm has already used them to devise a core set of resilient strategies that will work across a range of futures. That assumption is a sound starting point for technology planning, since the technology decisions will be coordinated from the outset with corporate priorities.

Now what? How can technology insights be derived from these scenarios?

Picking the Lineup. The next task is to pick managers who will participate in the technology-planning process. Effective leaders of the corporate-planning process can join this more-focused effort. Most scenario-based technology planning efforts also include members of the science and technology staff, marketers, business developers, manufacturing staff, and, occasionally, representatives of the finance staff. The team will be asked to learn to "live" in the futures that have been created. It will be their job to analyze and evaluate the new products that future customers will demand in each scenario. Then they must match those customer demands— the firm's potential future products—with appropriate technologies.

Two Methods for Adopting a World

There are two distinct approaches to this effort. In both, the planning teams break up into "world teams" and investigate the products demanded by customers in each scenario independently. At The Futures Group, we call this process *Adopt-A-World*™ because we ask each of the world teams to "adopt" a scenario world and assume for a time that it will be the only one that actually occurs.

Technology Linkages. In the first approach, all the products from all the scenarios are examined for technology linkages. The goal is to identify the core set of technologies that are required to develop the products that emerged from all the scenarios. This approach is certainly the most comprehensive, but it is also the most resource-intensive. Unfortunately, this approach does not provide technologists with a clear understanding of how their colleagues decide among various alternatives before making a product selection. The list of products that is collected is usually too much like a "wish list," and worse, this approach avoids answering the question, "What will you give up to get your wish?"

Technologies Needed for Tomorrow's Products. The second approach (see Exhibit 2), is more commonly used. First, a set of products that do not exist yet but probably will be needed in all the scenarios is identified. This set is then used to evaluate current technology alternatives. This process helps the technologists prioritize their own work and take into account corporate priorities. The goal is to select a core set of technologies that support customer needs in a range of futures, and that correspond to corporate goals. As is the case in all good scenario planning, this process should never be a onetime procedure, but a continuing part of the technology evaluation.

SCENARIO PLANNING IN THREE TYPES OF TECHNOLOGY-RELATED DECISIONS

There are numerous technology-related decisions that are enhanced by adopting scenario-based planning techniques. The following four case studies were selected to capture a range of applications for this techniques. In the first case, the scenario user, Consolidated Finance, was not a technology firm at all, but was making business decisions and investments based on which future technologies would succeed. The second case study looks at a more typical application of scenarios to technology decisions. In this case, the firm, The Knowledge Bank, used scenario-based planning to choose which technologies would form the foundation of new business processes (primarily "product" production and distribution). The third and fourth cases examine the technology decisions that firms—Industrial Visions and White Hat Aerospace—were required to meet future customer product needs at a time when their markets were in considerable turmoil and unusually unpredictable.

Exhibit 2
Technology Needed for Future Products

| Alternative Future Worlds | The Market in Each Scenario | Products and Services for Each Market | Robust Products and Services Viable Across the Scenario | Gap and Fit Analysis | Technology Expertise |

Technology Investment Priorities

Case Study: Consolidated Finance Invests in Technology Markets

This first case study may seem a bit out of place in this chapter because the company employing scenarios in this case was not a technology firm and had only rudimentary technology knowledge in-house. It is included for two reasons: First, technology is an ever more central feature of the global economy, and many different kinds of investment strategies require a technique for selecting among various technology investment opportunities. Second, this case study suggests that a scenario analysis can provide any organization with an "investment due diligence" tool that it can use to attract investment capital.

Consolidated Finance is a financial services firm with a strong regional base, a full range of services, and a national presence in a few niche markets in which it competes very successfully. Consolidated's introduction to scenario-based planning began with top management. The CEO had, over the past decade, driven the firm's growth with shrewd mergers and acquisitions. His strategy was to establish an unassailable position in:

- A select group of markets that corresponded to long-established core competencies in regionally-based products and services;

- High-volume transaction processing for a few select national customers.

By nearly every measure, the strategy was unfolding quite successfully and had several years of life remaining.

However, the CEO was concerned that the firm's management was becoming a bit complacent. Though the strategy was clearly understood by all the key executives, a noteworthy communications achievement, its execution had become a matter of "mere" operations and tactics. Additionally, he anticipated that the vision and goals of the original strategy—which was based on regional growth—was soon going to become a hindrance to expansive and innovative thinking. Consequently, Consolidated needed a new vision, new goals, and new strategies. Scenario-based planning was selected as the foundation process for developing new corporate strategic goals and strategies. The planning focus was, itself, quite expansive: To explore any and all potential financial services needs of society (with emphasis on Consolidated's current core competencies) across North America. The planning horizon was 10 years.

The planning process was moving along so successfully that about the time that the executives were involved in the Adopt-A-World exercises (before strategies had been developed), they decided to apply the scenarios to another, more immediate "bottom line" problem. Over the past five years, Consolidated had taken a rather large investment position in several areas of the transportation sector. The nature of the investments made Consolidated's position vulnerable to technology choices made in dozens of original equipment manufacturers (OEMs) and integration firms across the country over which they had no influence. Further, the long-term viability of transportation investments was affected by technologies outside of the transport sector—primarily in information processing and telecommunications. How safe were their investments? Should they reduce their commitment to some long-standing clients in this area?

After the addition of some transportation-relevant data into the scenarios, the executives of the transportation investment group engaged in an *Adopt-A-World*™ exercise of their own. This approach was a much more focused activity than the initial CEO-led effort. The goal of this project was to understand the consumer priorities in each scenario world and how they affect choices made about personal transportation alternatives and the logistics business that supplied consumer and retail delivery services. Consolidated recruited outside experts to help with the analysis of the technology implications of the range of future transportation needs.

The *Adopt-A-World*™ exercises revealed both critical transportation needs in North America over the next 10 years and some alternatives to conventional transportation. New concepts for vehicles and services that met those needs were identified, and the group ascertained which current and emerging technologies supported them. Finally, the current investment portfolio was compared to the list of technologies that supported transportation needs in a variety of scenarios. Consolidated managers had a pleasant surprise: Not only was their current technology investment strategy sound, but, if they brought in-house some specific technology and business expertise, they could safely increase their investments. It was also clear that those technology investments were vulnerable to sudden obsolescence as the decade passed. Therefore, Consolidated installed a technology tracking system and developed a hedging strategy. Finally, they evaluated various telecommunication alternatives—such as teleconferencing—as potential nontraditional competitors to transportation. As a result, the group recommended several technology investments to Consolidated's telecommunications investment group.

Case Study: Improving Business Process Technology

The Knowledge Bank (TKB) is an information services firm that had few real or potential competitors in its business area until the 1980s. TKB's competitive advantage rested on its expertise at converting raw government data into well-indexed information, and at efficiently publishing, distributing, and aggressively marketing the information. The firm's employment of scenario planning began with a technology-scanning project commissioned by a new president and a recently hired technology director. The business had not altered much since the 1920s, but suddenly a confluence of new technologies appeared to threaten the comfortably lethargic pace of change they had become used to over the decades.

The technology scan confirmed the company's fears and doubts. Developments in information-processing hardware, publishing and analytical software, and telecommunications signaled an approaching revolution for their industry. Particularly disturbing to TKB executives was the possibility that the barriers to entry in their niche business that once seemed so high might soon disappear.

Instead of predicting a new technology trend, the scanning effort had actually produced greater uncertainty throughout the company. The results of many of the technology scans seemed to point in different, often contradictory, directions. The research had produced only "possibilities" that "seemed" to portend threatening change. TKB executives had no method for testing or selecting from among the technology trends; they had no sense of coherent future direction. Which trends would dominate? Which would demand a large investment but never become a major market?

The Knowledge Bank decided to implement scenario-based planning to support its immediate decision-making and as an ongoing analysis process to test the relevance of emerging technologies. With scenarios developed, an *Adopt-A-World*™ approach (using the scenarios separately to derive alternative strategies, then synthe sizing the results into a core robust strategy) led TKB executives to recognize the potential of a significantly different business model.

The scenarios analysis of customer needs indicated that the intelligence-intensive analysis portion of TKB's information product would remain unassailable for at least another 10 years. Management did little to change this key source of competitive advantage. Instead, they moved their entire internal process of data coding, indexing, and analysis from paper and workshops to computers and e-mail. This process avoided undue disruption for employees who faced huge changes in their work, and avoided a reduction in the quality of the firm's product while the transition took place. TKB executives could afford to move deliberately because both customer interviews and scenario analysis of their customers' industries indicated that their best clients would themselves move slowly into the electronic data revolution. However, making a start at the transition process immediately was considered an important hedge for the potential success of expert system software.

Their new insight about their customers' future reactions led to another strategy. They brought their customers along with them as they explored electronic distribution of the product they would soon produce electronically. They not only codeveloped some of the distribution system with their customers, but set up education and training systems for their other clients. The scenario analysis of the future business environment led them to a sound and robust technology investment strategy. For example, they selected a combination of laser discs for yearly "publications" (although disc technology meant that it would be easy to produce them more often) plus an on-line service that could be inexpensively customized for individual client interests.

Many firms would have been pleased with achieving this much innovation, but key TKB executives understood just how lucky the company had been, and they were left with a sense that they had "caught it just in time." The president was determined that emerging technologies or unexpected shifts in the business environment would not catch them unaware in the future. A tracking system was established based on the combined use of scanning and scenarios. Technology trend scanning was initiated in conventional fashion, but an extra step was added to the analysis process. Each technology forecast or trend was "stress-tested" through the scenarios. This test asked the question, "What is the impact on TKB if this particular technology emerges in this particular scenario?" In a sense, the scenarios were used as a future "industry-relevance" filter to test for impact on TKB and to explore the impact of the trends in the set of scenarios.

The insights from this process flowed in two directions. The trends examined in the scanning process were often selected based upon scenario analysis. The following are two samples of how this analysis worked in practice:

- "Trend X turned out to have a huge impact on the regulatory environment in our industry in three of the scenarios. Get an outlook function for trend X set up in the scanning system."

- "Two of the scenarios implied an unmet customer need for self-diagnostic safety systems. Be sure to scan for emerging technologies that would enable them."

In other words, the scenarios are not just passive analytical tools for testing the relevance of emerging trends or technologies. They are also a source of insight into trends not yet on the horizon that should be included in the scanning process.

The system set up by TKB is simple and elegant. It has the virtue of being an ongoing process that keeps everyone thinking about technology in the context of scenario insights; it nicely reinforces the linkage between company strategy and technology investments. An additional advantage is that TKB executives will know quickly when the scenarios need revision.

TECHNOLOGIES FOR FUTURE PRODUCTS

Identifying future customer needs and selecting appropriate technologies for inclusion in new or modified products is perhaps the most powerful application of scenarios for technology planning. This process facilitates the identification of robust future customer needs—that is, those that will persist in a variety of future circumstances—thereby helping managers select the technologies most likely to be applicable in a wide range of future business environments. In our experience, companies that have adopted scenario technology planning have found that by developing strategic planning priorities derived from scenarios and prioritizing technology investments, they greatly increase their control over their own destiny. Scenario planning not only links technology decisions to future customer demand but forges strong ties between corporate strategy and the technology investments. Thus, technology choices are made within a strategic context that includes the new corporate vision, the market segments identified as most viable, long-range financial plans, and competitor assessment.

Case Study: Industrial Visions Tests the Viability of Its Recently Developed Products

Industrial Visions (IV) produces diagnostics equipment for manufacturing processes. Its product line was moderately successful in a very competitive market. The company recently completed an expensive R&D program intended to allow it to make it a quantum leap in performance over the competition. But, because of the surprising success of the research, Industrial Visions faced a propitious dilemma. Researchers had made two totally unexpected and quite dramatic breakthroughs, one in well-understood and commonly used analog sensor technology and the other in digital-scanning techniques.

To make matters more complicated, it seemed that either of these technologies could be successfully married to two newly developed image storage techniques, stable, high-resolution microfilm and digital electronic storage. All the combinations of new technology received enthusiastic support when explored with current clients. And, of course, all combinations had their internal supporters. Indeed, some serious factionalism within the firm was developing among the "preferred" approaches. However, there was only enough development money available for one combination.

Technology benchmarking measures that compared the new technology with all potential competitors in forecasted performance growth were not decisive, and customer focus groups gave no useful selection criteria. To resolve this quandary, the vice president for R&D decided to see if a scenario examination of future market conditions would provide some insight. He was skeptical, but the CEO suggested such an approach. In fact, the CEO was considering using scenarios for strategic planning, and thought this technology decision might make a good test of the technique.

Some unique characteristics of the market concerning the motivations of their customers' customers, plus the need to explore global opportunities and threats made the study complicated enough to require seven scenarios.

Although an unusually high number, it was not an unworkable one because the managers wanted to stress-test their new technology combinations, not invent new product ideas.

Industrial Visions' top management was in for a number of surprises. First, they did get several unexpected new product ideas from exploring the future priorities of their customers' customers. Second, they got a much keener appreciation for the potential market strengths of one of their competitors. This competitor was a rival that they had previously wrongly tended to dismiss as "second string." Third, they ended up spending a bit more money than originally intended because they chose two technology combinations.

The scenario analysis of the manufacturing diagnostics market for their equipment in the developing countries indicated a far larger, faster growing and more robust market than trend-based market analyses had forecast. However, this market featured unique conditions. Less-educated employees, difficult climate conditions, and poorly performing power-generating equipment in this "emerging markets" sector pointed to the need for more rugged, easier-to-use, and easier-to-repair digital equipment. But this equipment would be more expensive. On the other hand, Adopt-A-World scenario analysis of the advanced industrial markets in the United States, Western Europe, and Japan indicated a strong tendency to prefer the best sensor resolution possible at the lowest price—a combination of preferences that implied the market would choose film-based sensors. Conversely, several of the scenarios indicated that future environmental regulations could restrict the film-based approach because it required several hard-to-dispose-of industrial chemicals. For the advanced industrial markets, the high-resolution analog system was married to the digital storage approach; but digital technology was a long-term hedge in the event that restrictive environmental regulations were enacted.

Industrial Visions' final decision was:

- Digital storage for both markets;

- Analog sensors in the advanced industrial markets;

- Digital sensors in the developing countries;

- A new strategic alliance with that competitor that had seemed second string.

Since implementing that decision, Industrial Vision has gained some market share in the advanced industrial markets—it grows modestly, while all competitors but one stagnate—and it now dominates its market in the developing countries.

Case Study: Corporate Scenarios Employed to Prioritize Technology Investments

White Hat Aerospace is a defense company with expertise in air-launched missiles, communications, and several other defense technology areas. A year ago, it completed a corporate-wide scenario-based strategic-planning project. The first application of scenarios analyzed the overall business portfolio of the company, during which the scenario team studied future markets but not in great detail. The planning effort had resolved many market priorities and corporate organizational issues. Three businesses were sold off and a foreign infrared sensor firm was acquired.

Exhibit 3
Using Scenarios to Identify Core Technologies

| Alternative Future Scenario | Markets in Each Scenario | Products and Services in Each Market | Robust Products | Analysis of Robust Products | Core Technologies across a Range of Products |

A new *Adopt-A-World*[TM] exercise began with a focused look at future combat missions and future customer needs 15 years out. About 25 new product ideas that seemed viable across the scenarios emerged from the process. Seven of the new products were missiles—three air-to-air and four air-to-ground. White Hat managers had to decide which missiles to invest in, given reduced defense spending and limited corporate resources.

But, if you have seven potential products—in this case, missiles—how do you select the right one to produce? The first step is the one taken by White Hat, and it follows the scenario philosophy of managing uncertainty. Technology roadmaps were developed for all seven missiles. A sensitivity test was run to find the core technologies across all the missiles. That core set of technologies, those that would be needed regardless of the missile chosen, became the priority technology investments (see Exhibit 3).

White Hat would first choose the missiles to be developed in four years. Some years later it would have to impose a technology freeze—a point at which key component technologies must be "set in stone" so that production requiring long lead time could begin. The company would impose the freeze in six or seven years. The time preceding the freeze was used to hone the scenario analysis, involve clients in that analysis, and run classic mission studies on the missiles. Eventually, four missiles were chosen for development, and one of these projects was subsequently canceled. Additionally, several current production missiles from several competing manufacturers have now been required to incorporate White Hat's new technologies into ongoing missile upgrade and modification programs.

CONCLUSIONS

Scenario-based planning for technology decisions can be a powerful tool to manage the uncertainties that surround important technology investments. The scenarios provide managers with a window on potential future market needs, a tool for systematic and innovative consideration of new customer needs, and a method for evaluating the long-term viability of current product ideas or technology developments. The scenarios help you to set market-driven priorities on your technology investment plans so they are more than just a lengthy wish list.

However, the greatest leverage will come from incorporating technology scenario planning into your regular ongoing planning process. Scenario planning offers managers a powerful new way of thinking about their business future with its myriad unpredictable opportunities and threats. Managers who have "rehearsed" various technologies futures will be better prepared to address discontinuous change than their competitors. They will react faster and with a greater sense of confidence. That capability is a meaningful competitive advantage.

AMAZON.PLAGUE

SUMMARY

The world of 2020 looks bleak. Since 2010, the globe has been swept by highly contagious, deadly viruses that flare up, die down and return in mutated form. The world economy has declined sharply as trade and commerce have dried up, and is now mired in a serious, long-term recession. Many nations have become either authoritarian, ruled by demagogic strongmen, or simply succumbed to chaos. The U.S. is among a handful of countries fortunate enough to have resilient political structures and relatively low fatality rates. These countries have signed a mutual assistance treaty to find a cure for the viruses and protect national security. The "viable states" have sealed their borders, but they are constantly threatened by mass migration attempts from less fortunate neighbors. In the U.S., the traditional Democratic and Republican parties have been replaced by the Greens and the Techs; the former look to a return to basic living and tend to blame technology for the world's current evils, while the latter look to medical research and technology to solve the current crisis. Power increasingly resides in community groups and local health centers, most of which are connected to and supported by the federal government. The public has generally agreed to sacrifice some personal freedoms in favor of medical IDs and increased surveillance of potentially "unhealthy" populations. The internet has evolved into the Global Information Grid (GIG), which is the preferred method of purchasing, communication and education, allowing people to avoid large groups and crowded areas. It is one of the few unambiguous signs of progress in this world.

"Why is the checkpoint always crowded when I'm in a hurry?" thought Samantha Hernandez as she inched her AT (automated transport) forward toward the gate. There were at least five other ATs ahead of her. That was one of the problems with leaving the enclave. "I'll miss Dr. Tucker's lecture", she thought. Oh well, nothing she could do about that now. She could always watch it later on archive, but she preferred to catch it in real time to take part in the discussion.

Samantha, or Sam as she was often called, looked out the window of the AT. The sky was a deep blue, the blue of spring or fall. The colorful trees swayed in the breeze and the mountains stood cool and majestic in the distance. "What a beautiful view", she thought, choosing to ignore the ruins of a nearby town off to the left. Too bad you couldn't open that window to feel the breeze. Then she reconsidered. It was just as well – there were reports of new Java strains in that ruined town a couple of months ago. Better to wait 'til I'm back in the enclave.

Finally, she reached the checkpoint gate, turned in her AT for disinfection and entered the AntiViro Chamber. She swiped her MedID over the Identipatch. *Samantha Hernandez, resident, number 353*, said a disembodied voice in the chamber. The robot scanner slowly took a readout. Sam closed her eyes and tried to relax. She'd been scanned a hundred times before but always felt that frisson of fear, waiting for the alarm bells to go off and tell her she was infected. She'd seen it happen, too, people taken off in auto-quarantine, never to be seen again. She knew more than one person who carried suicide pills to avoid the agony of a slow, painful death by virus.

The green light above the door flashed and the door slid open into the enclave. Sam breathed a sigh of relief and walked toward her house, waving at Jack, the Community Security Liaison in the protective booth near the checkpoint. She looked at her watch. "Cool", she thought. "I won't miss the lecture in real time after all."

The soft, clear tones of the MoniTV AVR (accurate voice reproduction) came through: *"Introductory lecture of Socio-epidemiology 101 class. Real-time commlink/video format. September 5, 2020. Dr. Stephen Tucker of National Online University."* Dr. Tucker came on screen. He was smiling, but looked pale, and beads of sweat dotted his forehead through the makeup. "I wonder what's up with him", Sam thought. She couldn't know that Dr. Tucker had, because of a circuit malfunction at NOU's Remote Studio, just been incorrectly diagnosed as HIR (high infection risk) and trapped in the AntiViro Chamber for 10 minutes. All his worst nightmares about dying horribly and alone had been lived out in that 10 minutes and he had not had much time to regroup himself before the lecture started. He wiped his brow and spoke.

"Good morning, class. Or, I should say, hello, given that many of you are 'attending' this lecture at other times of the day. Welcome to Socio-epidemiology 101 at National Online University. For some of you, this is a required core course in the pre-med major, Epidemiology/Virology concentration. For many others, this course is part of your training as Community Protection Liaisons for your particular community or enclave. All of you taking this course need to pay careful attention to what is taught, especially because that information could mean the difference between life and death for you, your family, your neighbors and your future patients. To get credit for attending this lecture, please press the virtual button on the bottom right of your MoniTV and then swipe your MedID across the IdentiPatch that appears.

In this class, we will cover the basic biological structures of three viruses and their known variant strains. We will also learn the basic epidemiological precepts of how these viruses are thought to have originated, their vectors, how they multiply within their hosts and are transferred to new hosts, and the symptoms of viral diseases. Perhaps most importantly, we will cover the essential procedures for avoiding and/or quarantining the viruses. As you know, the GIG is a vital tool in the containment and information management process.

Before we start into the main part of this course, however, I feel it is imperative that I give you a solid overview of the events of the last twenty or so years. The events of this time period are key to understanding the almost overwhelming challenges we face today. Many of you were very young when the viruses we will study first appeared, and have very little memory of life before the First Pandemic. To understand the biology and epidemiology of these viruses, it is vital that you understand the societal context in which they first appeared and began to wreak havoc. Our response to the viral outbreaks was as much sociopolitical as it was medical; hence the course title, Socio-epidemiology. Please tell your MoniTV to switch to high resolution so you can see the graphics I have prepared for this session.

At the risk of sounding preachy, I want to give you this introduction as a warning lesson, a lesson against human arrogance. It may be hard to believe, but before 2009 the world, and especially the medical community, thought we had tamed infectious disease and would never again see the like of the so-called "Spanish Flu" of 1918. Viral outbreaks occurred in isolated areas and quickly died out with the deaths of their hosts. While some epidemiologists could conceive of larger outbreaks, they believed they were easily contained and managed. And they believed that the main cause for concern was drug-resistant strains of TB and pneumonia, especially in overcrowded prisons and hospitals in inner cities and the developing world. The events of the last 20 years have laid these false beliefs to rest, and shown us just how far we are from 'conquering' disease."

"Blah blah blah," said Samantha out loud. "I thought this was science, not history! When do we get to the good stuff?"

The World of 1999 – 2005 flashed in large letters on the screen as Dr. Tucker began speaking again.

"Ironically, the world at the end of 1999 was obsessed with a completely different kind of virus. Everyone wondered what would happen to the world's computers as the clock struck midnight on January 1, 2000. The infamous 'Y2K bug' was alternately trumpeted as the root of the coming apocalypse and dismissed as nothing to worry about. Given these two extreme viewpoints, the end result was bound to fall somewhere in between. Y2K was certainly not as bad as the doomsayers predicted, nor was it completely harmless. Airlines, shipping companies and local utilities, among others, suffered temporarily paralyzing meltdowns during January and February. These disruptions were felt more in the emerging markets than in the developed world, but they had an impact everywhere. Together, these impacts were significant enough to cause a mild global recession in early 2000.

The world economy recovered from this recession in just six months. While the U.S. economy was soon growing at a fast pace, many of the emerging markets began to play catch-up. A new round of reforms in Southeast Asia and Latin America spurred new capital investment from Japan (itself reforming its financial structures) and the West. New production facilities in emerging markets began to demand more natural resources as raw material. Emerging markets began to trade more with each other as well as to export goods to developed nations. Growth in the world economy also led to new technology investment, particularly in the internet, as e-business took off and everyone clamored for wider bandwidth and faster service.

Recession next hit the world economy in 2003. Falling demand from western markets was partially compensated for in emerging countries by demand from their own growing middle class. More and more capital flowed into and around Southeast Asia and Latin America. This accelerated industrial development contributed to an immense hunger for resources and thus an increasing rate of environmental degradation. All of the economic growth and new wealth in emerging markets did little to curb infectious diseases such as dengue fever, malaria and Hanta virus, and contributed to the steadily rising rate of pollution-related fatalities. China alone counted at least 400,000 fatalities resulting from air and water pollution, while Russia was losing thousands to TB and pneumonia every year. Africa benefited somewhat from renewed economic investment, but AIDS and HIV continued to ravage countries south of the Sahara.

The U.S. presidential election of 2004 ushered in a conservative Republican who campaigned on a platform of economic growth via increased support for corporations and a comprehensive plan for deregulation. I should say here that this was an exceptionally mediocre year for politicians—even in a recession, the best and the brightest were migrating to the private sector, not politics. This trend continued 'til only a handful of really top people populated Congress in 2008. Soon after the Republican president's inauguration, environmental laws came under attack from the White House and Congress. The federal government's scope was further scaled back. Corporations, armed with new government subsidies and tax breaks, invested still more in overseas emerging markets. Rapacious demand for raw materials in those markets increased industrial forays into rainforests, river deltas and other resource-rich areas."

"Jeez, what do politics in 2004 have to do with viruses in 2021?" wondered Samantha, doodling on her electronic notebook as The World of 2005 – 2010 appeared on the MoniTV.
"Over the next two years, the world economy grew at an impressive

rate, again particularly in the emerging market areas," said Dr. Tucker. "While viral outbreaks and pollution continued to take their toll in these areas, they caused only the slightest tremor in emerging economies. Internet technology, under its latest incarnation as the Supranet, continued to advance, fueled by e-business and cheap access to wide bandwidth. The Supranet made affordable, real-time videoconferencing widely available and increasingly used in businesses and by consultants to cut costs. Individuals were soon investing in this technology. T1 and cable lines had become cheap and commonplace and companies were exploring uncharted territory in wireless connectivity.

By 2006, shifts in the global climate started to become noticeable, mostly in the form of varying weather patterns. There was a good deal of debate about whether these shifts were symptoms of global warming (as Greens and liberals proclaimed) or merely a blip in the natural weather cycle (as the conservative power structure in the U.S. continued to assert). The scientific community remained divided. The White House and Congress, now increasingly opinion poll driven, refused to act on the matter as long as the U.S. public was OK and enjoying its prosperity. Reacting to what it saw as a crisis in the making, the Green Party began to mobilize in Europe and the U.S. in an effort to gather support around the issue. A new business cycle of mild recession and quick recovery occurred in 2008. As the world economy rebounded, however, new scientific evidence showed that the world was generally becoming a bit warmer and wetter. As in 2006, this evidence was hotly debated in the political arena. What was hard to debate, though, were the documented increases in the rodent and insect populations worldwide and the appearance of new strains of drug-resistant infectious diseases, particularly in Latin America, Africa and Southeast Asia, but also to a lesser degree in the U.S. and Europe.

Based on this evidence, the Green movement began to enjoy a resurgence in Europe as people grew increasingly worried about environmental degradation and disease. The Greens also gained some popularity in the States; although the conservative Republican candidate was narrowly re-elected president in 2008, several members of the Green Party were elected to Congress that same year. In an interesting departure from previous doctrine, a branch of the U.S. Greens began to incorporate a strong anti-technology agenda into their platforms, under the perception that technology was largely responsible for the degradation, resource depletion and new strains of therapy-resistant disease. While some Greens supported this anti-technology agenda, others preferred to focus on the environmental aspect of the movement."

The World of 2010 – 2014 appeared on screen. "This is the good part", thought Sam, then looked around guiltily as if she'd been caught doing something naughty.

Dr. Tucker's voice became more solemn. "The First Pandemic hit the world full force in 2010. The first news of the plague came in reports from South America during the last months of 2009, which said that a 'new Ebola virus' had appeared and was spreading throughout the continent. Epidemiologists studying the situation claimed that, like Ebola, this new virus was too 'virulent' to spread beyond a limited population, and would die off quickly if minimal public health measures were taken to avoid contact with the bodily fluids of the sick. They produced computer models to this effect, published not only in medical journals but in popular newsweeklies and the Supranet. The public was reassured, but only temporarily. By the end of 2009, more than 5 million people had died in South America alone and thousands were getting sick and dying in other parts of the world.

By March 2010, it became clear that we were in the midst of a viral pandemic, the scale of which was unknown to recent history. Thousands of people in almost every country were dying horrible deaths, despite never having had contact with vectors or the bodily fluids of sick people. Scientists and doctors soon realized that unlike most other deadly viruses, such as Ebola and Hanta, this new virus was highly contagious and could be spread human to human through airborne and/or aerosol contact. We will learn more about these terms during this course. It also had a much longer dormancy period than other viral hemorrhagic fevers (VHFs); victims of the virus often did not show symptoms for two or three e

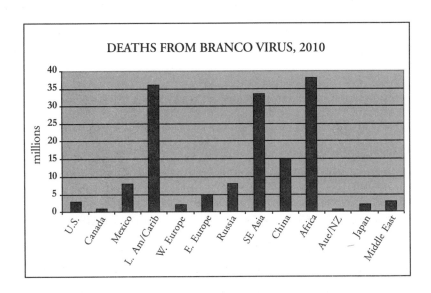

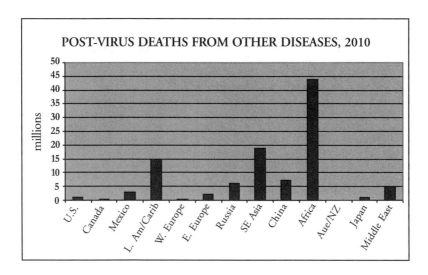

POST-VIRUS DEATHS FROM OTHER DISEASES, 2010

weeks after infection. Thus, it was much easier to spread the virus unknowingly through travel and daily contact with others.

The symptoms of the new virus, soon called Branco Virus after the Brazilian river near which it was thought to have originated, were horrible but confusing. When symptoms finally did appear after the dormancy period, for the first 3 – 5 days they mimicked those of a bad cold or flu, with a cough, runny nose, fever and headache. Then symptoms worsened and included violent coughing, difficulty breathing and extremely high fever. In some cases, patients bled into the skin and other organs, a symptom often associated with septicemic plague. Patients usually died within 10 days of first showing symptoms, with plenty of time to infect others in their homes, communities and health care facilities.

During 2010 alone, over 150 million people died worldwide as a direct result of the virus. Most of the fatalities occurred in the emerging markets, but 4 million people died in the U.S., 3 million in Western Europe and 2 million in Japan. In addition, another

100 million of those who did not die from the virus were weakened so severely that they died of pneumonia, TB, flu and other normally less threatening diseases. Here are the statistics by region. You can retain them for later viewing by entering VC (voice command) 'Retain Branco Charts.'"

Two colorful charts appeared on screen for a couple of minutes. Sam stared at them intently.

Dr. Tucker continued. "The Branco Virus tended to prey on the malnourished, the weak and the sick, as well as those living in crowded, unsanitary conditions with little or no access to healthcare. Naturally, then, many of the fatalities occurred among the urban poor in the megacities of the developing world, and in the shanty towns that often outskirted those cities. But many also died in more rural areas; reports came from Africa of entire villages being wiped out in a matter of weeks. In the U.S., the urban poor of the inner cities and the elderly were hit hardest by the disease. Everywhere health care systems were stretched to the limit, especially because the medical community was trying to cope with a relatively high fatality rate as well. International organizations such as the WHO and the U.N. tried to curb Branco's spread, but the best they could do under the circumstances was to institute quarantine procedures, distribute basic preventive gear and pour money into anti-virus research.

It is difficult to describe the magnitude of the problem or the nature of the panic that set in as the year progressed and more and more people died. Now that we have been living with the viruses for 10 years, we are more accustomed to the impact they have had on our lives. But in 2010, people had a hard time simply imagining a pandemic of that size, much less experiencing the aftershocks for themselves."

Samantha nodded, reliving her own childhood memories. She'd been eight when Branco had hit, but could still remember vividly the panic in her hometown of Columbus, her mother taking her out of school, the vaccinations, her home schooling. Her reverie was disrupted by Dr. Tucker.

"In many of the developing countries hardest hit by the pandemic," he continued, "social interaction dissolved into chaos as more and more people died. Fear and distrust of others became part of daily life, exacerbating existing ethnic and religious tensions and bringing old international conflicts back to the fore. Many countries claimed bio warfare attack and pointed to their neighbors as the source of the disease. Civil society degenerated and governments fell, to be replaced either by strongmen spewing demagoguery or by anarchy. In other countries less affected by the virus, governments struggled to keep the civil structures from falling into chaos. This wasn't easy."

Samantha shuddered as pictures appeared on the MoniTV of riots and lootings in Baghdad and Bogota, and averted her eyes at images of piles of corpses stacked in African villages and on street corners in Jakarta, Lima and Shenzen.

"The fact that the U.S. was not as badly affected by the virus as the developing world should not obscure the reality of its 4 million fatalities during 2010. Health care facilities were strained to the limit, in some places with the sick, in others with countless paranoid patients with psychosomatic 'symptoms.' Parents kept their children out of school to protect them from Branco and any illness that would increase their susceptibility. Cities faced heretofore unseen public health crises. Some packed up and moved to more sparsely populated areas, while others rioted for protection or a nonexistent 'vaccine.' A wave of panic washed over the nation as people demanded that the government do something to protect citizens from the virus. The Democrats and Republicans tried their best to respond to the crisis but with a drastically pared down federal infrastructure and no unified policymaking procedure, they were ill-equipped to deal with such an unexplored and unanticipated threat to national and global security.

The 2010 Congressional elections were ugly and contentious all over the country, as candidates on both sides used increasingly negative rhetoric to slam their opponents and play on the fears of their constituents. The Green Party gained a large measure of support for its pro-nature, anti-technology platform, and 10 more Greens were elected into the House. A small group of Democrats and Republicans with some medical knowledge and an understanding of the crisis at hand formed a new alliance in early 2011. Calling themselves the Technologists, or Techs for short, they coalesced around the idea of shifting new resources toward the medical and biotech establishment in an effort to find a cure for the virus. This philosophy came in direct conflict with that of the Greens, and soon the two groups were battling it out on the floors of Congress. The few remaining Democrats and Republicans were soon marginalized, and began to realize that their conservative vs. liberal brand of politicking was irrelevant to the crisis of the day.

By 2011, as you might well imagine, the world economy had taken a dramatic downturn. International trade declined sharply, increasingly shunned by populations who worried that virus vectors or droplets would be present in goods shipments. Unemployment rose as trade and commerce fell. Even domestic commerce fell as people curtailed their shopping in an effort to prevent infection. Factories faced a severe labor shortage as workers died or were afraid to congregate in enclosed spaces. Countries saw their economies contract as fear and death continued to spread unabated.

The Branco Virus ran its course and by 2012 people had either succumbed to it or gained some immunity to it. But no one was ready to breathe a sigh of relief and go back to 'normal life.' In fact, the concept of normal life had changed dramatically for everyone. While by this time very few people were dying of the virus, its economic, political and social aftereffects were still overwhelming. The world economy was still declining rapidly. Governments were straining to keep order and to find ways of stimulating growth that would avoid contamination. An atmosphere of fear and distrust pervaded society. Anyone who looked unhealthy, tired or simply 'different' was shunned and feared.

The unevenness with which the Branco Virus had affected the world's countries triggered a massive population shift as people sought refuge from violence, chaos and illness. The U.S. and Europe in particular felt forced to close their borders to limit immigration from Asia and Latin America. The U.S. faced a daunting problem on its southern border; Mexico's fatality rate, at 8% of its population, was much higher than that of the U.S., and people were desperate to leave. New physical barriers and health stations were erected along the Rio Grande in an effort to control the number of immigrants crossing the border and to test them for disease. Those who could pay to fly into the U.S. were required to spend 30 days in special quarantine facilities before they were allowed to enter the country. These facilities were at first temporary structures and then permanent buildings, paid for by the fees generated from the prospective immigrants.

As the dust cleared from the Branco Virus and people began assessing the damage, the Greens all over the world began gaining support. In the U.S. election of 2012 they continued amassing seats in Congress. But they were counterbalanced by the Techs, who, with the support of the medical and scientific communities, also sent a number of representatives to Congress. The U.S. economy attempted a feeble recovery as new health care industries surfaced and new disinfection methods were introduced. Everywhere survivors took an almost guilty sigh of relief, but everyone wondered uneasily where or when, or whether, the next 'plague' would strike."

Samantha sat glued to the MoniTV, her electronic doodles forgotten as The World of 2014 – 2020 appeared. Dr. Tucker cleared his throat, took a sip of Ultra C Immunoboost, and continued.

"They didn't have to wait long. In early 2014 the first news of the 'Asian Branco' surfaced on the Supranet. Thought to have originated in the Indonesian rainforest, the virus was multi-strained and deadly, with the same highly contagious airborne infection transmittal as the Amazon virus. Spreading quickly throughout Southeast Asia into China and India, the virus reached Europe via the Middle

East and the U.S. through a boatload of Chinese immigrants that secretly came ashore in Southern California. Soon the virus spread through every continent except Antarctica, and by 2016 over 250 million had died of the Indo virus, 9 million of those in the United States.

This second cycle of disease was even more devastating than the first. Governments that had barely managed to keep order during the Branco virus pandemic were swept away by the Indo strain. The world economy, still laboring under the impact and aftershocks of the first virus, tumbled further as most international trade dried up and production of even essential goods was cut drastically. The second pandemic gave rise to a new class of snake oil salesmen capitalizing on the crisis to sell 'cures' and 'virus shots' to panicking populations. This was outlawed by Congress in 2017 and, as you know, is now monitored by the government and the Community On-line Liaisons.

More countries eagerly accepted the rise of finger-pointing demagogues eager to pin the 'blame' for the pandemics on their less badly affected neighbors. In the Middle East, the ultra fundamentalist regime in Iran took over a weakened Iraq and Afghanistan as part of a greater 'Democratic Republic of Islam,' or DRI. It claimed that Israel had started the virus to kill Muslims and thus had to be punished. This put Israel on high alert; it moved to martial law and constructed new barriers along the Jordan. Japan and Taiwan were similarly under siege from desperate Southeast Asians whose unscrupulous leaders, looking for a way to shift blame from themselves, called on them to exact revenge on those countries for 'cooking up' the virus.

The urgent calls from Tel Aviv, Taipei and Tokyo woke up Washington from its isolationist stupor. Supported by the medical and scientific communities, the Techs fielded as their presidential candidate a competent, charismatic epidemiologist who'd been in the trenches of the virus war for the last five years. She campaigned on a platform of cooperation, bringing the world's best researchers and medical professionals together to find real vaccinations and cures against viruses. While still arguing for the need for medical certificates for entry into the U.S., she also asserted that the country's isolationist stance was ineffective against viral spread and cut it off from the possibility of medical breakthroughs. Only working with our allies and pooling our best technology, she said, will we resolve this crisis.

Her opponent was a Green with a streak of populism who claimed that if elected, he would parcel out government land to the healthy so they could 'start again.' He also claimed that technology had caused the 'plagues' and they would only be eradicated by radically cutting industrial production and technological oppression of the planet. The race was close, and the outcome was hotly contested (it was the first election held over the Supranet and there were many technical glitches in the vote count), but the Tech candidate was narrowly elected President. The post-election polls and comments from voters, however, made it clear that they would hold her to her promises of finding a solution to the pandemics.

The first move of the new Tech White House after the inauguration in 2017 was to push through legislation providing funds to strengthen and revamp the Supranet. The Supranet had already become (as the GIG is today) the U.S.'s vital communication and commerce channel, linking remaining businesses with consumers and each other, and providing news updates to those in isolated communities. This legislation resulted in the planning and construction of the Global Information Grid, which as you know is the backbone of our society today. I should comment here that 'Global' is a rather optimistic word, given that much of the world is still in chaos and very little reliable news is available from those countries hard hit by disease. But 'Global' at this point includes countries from every continent around the world. You can enter VC 'GIG Members' to download a full list of GIG member countries."

Dr. Tucker stopped to wipe his forehead, and Sam again reflected that he looked pale. He took a deep breath and continued speaking.

"In 2018, a variant strain of the Indo virus, called the Java virus, appeared, to which a number of survivors of the 2014-2016 pandemic were not immune. Scientists believe the virus underwent an *antigenic shift*, mutating so rapidly that very few people remained immune. We will study antigenic shifts in detail later on in this course. 25 million people died that year, half a million of those in the U.S. That year, the U.S. and its allies signed a treaty of mutual assistance, pledging to coordinate anti-virus efforts and to share (without thought of profit or gain) any vaccine or cure with other treaty members and the world. The treaty also contained a promise to help protect other members from rogue states. The scientific and medical teams got to work on their research, often working remotely with their colleagues in other countries. Elite U.S. MedSec teams from the armed forces were dispatched to protect citizens, border areas and coastal zones in Asian, Middle Eastern and

European member nations. They worked jointly with WHO-CDC task forces that focused on disease control and treaty member certification.

The president's Viral Epidemiology Commission (VEC) submitted a report in late 2018 asserting the likelihood of a regular cycle of viral mutation and epidemic which would continue to kill millions around the world if a solution were not found. Armed with this report, the president went live over the GIG with her 2019 State of the Union address. Stressing the need to find a cure, she called for increased government and private spending on medical research. Her other fiscal priorities, she said, would be agriculture, water treatment, information technology including robotics, individual and group prophylactics, and security for communities and the nation. We only have a short time to beat these viruses, she said.

The double-edged meaning of her statement was clear – the threat was not only from disease, but also from the anti-technology ultra-Greens, who would gain more influence if the Tech mandate were not fulfilled. After a fiercely competitive campaign, the Techs were returned to office in 2020 to continue their work against virus and disease. The Techs, and those of us in the medical community, face enormous challenges, posed not only by the mutation cycle of the viruses but also by the radical Greens. The Greens are at best skeptical of what we are trying to accomplish and at worst openly antagonistic."

Dr. Tucker sighed and took a sip of Immunoboost as the word Today flashed across the screen.

"Let me bring this lecture to a close with a snapshot of the world we live in today, a snapshot which will give you some context for your SEP 101 course material. It is a bleak picture, and demonstrates the importance of what we will be studying over the next 14 weeks. The U.S. domestic picture is mixed. Our relatively well prepared public health system and our resilience in the face of crisis have meant that the viruses have not affected us as drastically as other, less fortunate, societies. It is sad but true to say that we have been lucky to lose only 15 million of our citizens over the last ten years. Many other regions have suffered much worse. However, that has not saved our society from becoming the highly-divisive and fragmented entity it is today.

The struggle between the Techs and the Greens in Congress is mirrored in U.S. society. Some of us have turned to science and technology to solve this urgent problem, while others point to them as the root cause of the illness, misery and desperation so prevalent in the world today. New political power has accrued to local health centers, which control disease spread and work directly with at-risk populations, and Community Liaisons, which as you know are responsible for security, communication, prophylactics and disinfection in all communities and enclaves except those of the ultra-Greens.

Many of those in Congress today are doctors and scientists, representing the increased power of health care in our society.

The rift has widened between the more moderate Greens and their radical counterparts. The ultra-Green movement has gained momentum in several western states, establishing its own settlements and accusing the government and scientific community of all manner of misdeeds, from planting the initial Branco virus in South America to repressing free American citizens to 'raping' the Earth for profit. The movement has turned against technology, using simpler equipment to farm and maintain its settlements. However, it is not averse to exploiting the ubiquity of the GIG for its own benefit! The more radical members are thought to be responsible for the SB Merck Pfizer bombing last year, the destruction of three health centers and the poison gas attack on VEC headquarters earlier this summer that killed 17 and sickened 84.

The U.S. economy is in the midst of a ten-year downturn, and has suffered serious shocks in response to the events of the last decade. Gross domestic product has declined steadily as trade and commerce have dropped off, and unemployment and inflation are higher than they have been since the Great Depression of the 1930s. Indeed, our economic situation is not unlike that of the 1930s, with some important differences. The only semblance of a global economy exists among the viable states, and even then physical trade is highly restricted to essential goods, such as disinfected agricultural products, technology and medical supplies.

The only real bright spot in our economy today is the virtual marketplace. The GIG has been the backbone of the economy and society since it was established, as was its previous incarnation, the Supranet. It allows people to communicate and buy what they need online, without exposing themselves to the risk of infection.

Business-to-business and business-to-consumer transactions take place almost entirely over the GIG (it's a good thing e-business really took off here after 2004!). Encryption technology has been buttressed after recent threats to the GIG by ultra-Green offshoots in Montana, Colorado and Missouri. Someone actually has to make the stuff we buy and sell; all the factories and industrial facilities here are now WHO-9000 certified, which means they have the highest disinfection and disease prevention standards. While the U.N. continues to operate, the WHO is now the most important international organization. The U.N. often coordinates its military security efforts with WHO programs.

The growth areas in the U.S. economy are few. Obviously the information technology sector is growing rapidly, especially in the areas of remote diagnostics, remote security sensing and robotics. The IT is working closely with the medical/scientific community and the government on products deemed critical to national security and health. High-tech firms have also joined with medical supply companies to manufacture and sell prophylactic materials, not only to the medical establishment but also to the general public. Miraculously, our agricultural sector was not seriously affected by the viruses and continues to flourish, with a focus on high-yield, genetically modified foods. While these growth areas don't exactly make up for the myriad economic disruptions of the last decade, they do help us avoid a more serious and permanent depression. And the American people's buying patterns have shifted from a high-consumption, luxury-loving lifestyle to one that values adequate, essential, good-quality items – 'The Basics.'"

Dr. Tucker paused and then asked the students watching in real-time if they had any comments about the lecture or about the world they lived in. A man in his forties came on screen.

"You know, the ultra-Greens do have a point about repressing citizens," he said. "Compared to 1999 or even 2009, we do have fewer personal freedoms now. We have voluntarily restricted our own rights to freedom of movement and assembly, and voluntarily accepted more government interference in our daily lives. Think of the number of times a day you are required to swipe your MedID, even in your own home, or walk through a AntiViro chamber if you go out, or submit to Securicam surveillance in high-risk areas."

Dr. Tucker responded, "I agree with you, but I would venture to say that these measures were only set up in response to our ongoing catastrophe and its attendant social repercussions, and have been instrumental in keeping our disease and fatality rates relatively low. Most people (with the notable exception of the ultra-Greens) have been willing to limit their freedoms in exchange for an increased sense of security, from both the viruses and their social effects, for themselves and their families."

A girl about Sam's age appeared on screen. "I saw a program on the GIG that said that Branco was started in a lab in Pennsylvania. Could some of this virus activity be bio warfare?"

"Well, the natural biological threat is compounded by the threat of manmade biological agents," replied Dr. Tucker. People everywhere are fearful of bio warfare. Some here and overseas blame the U.S. and its allies for the spread of Branco, Indo and Java, while some terrorist groups overseas have actually taken credit for unleashing the viruses! All I can say is, the scientific community insists that the viruses evolved naturally, and as a member of that community, I believe it. Many of us worry, though, that rogue nations could use bio warfare under cover of a naturally occurring disease. This is why our government and private sector assets abroad have been shut down except for those in the treaty member states."

"However, I would argue that much of today's threat to the U.S. stems from the social ramifications of disease and economic downturn. The viruses have weakened organized crime, especially in Latin America and Asia, but localized, individual crime has increased dramatically. Personal weapons have proliferated throughout the world and security is a dominant societal issue, especially in urban areas and other economically distressed enclaves. Survival crime is up – the urban poor seek desperately needed food and medical supplies. With demand for essential goods high and supply low, informal black markets have sprung up all over the country."

The girl on screen nodded. "Just this morning I saw a story over *GIG News* about government security forces breaking up an illegal network selling oxygen mini-pumps and contraband individual viral filtration systems," she said.

Sam entered VC "Participate" and suddenly Dr. Tucker was looking at her. "Dr. Tucker," she began, "What about those other countries, outside the treaty zone?" She was still haunted by the pictures of piled bodies in African villages.

Dr. Tucker sighed. "Well, I'm sorry to say, the outlook for the non-treaty world is even bleaker than it is here. Disease, economic depression, political chaos and regional instability have made life in most countries absolutely miserable. All of these countries (as well as the U.S.) are under extreme social pressure and many are in anarchy. Tribal wars in Africa are finishing the work the viruses have started. The Mahgreb countries have not been hit as hard by disease as sub-Saharan Africa, but they have come under the influence of ultra-fundamentalist groups subsidized by the DRI. Authoritarian rule is becoming the norm in Eastern Europe and the Balkans. Just yesterday I received a preliminary report of a rogue Chinese division marching on Korea."

He scratched his head and continued. "And so you see now why our work in this course is so important, and why it is so important that we find a solution to this crisis. Life in so many places around the globe has reverted to its Hobbesian state, and it threatens to become 'nasty, brutish and short' for the remaining strongholds. It is up to us in the viable states to find a cure and vaccination for these scurrilous viruses, so that we can reconstruct the world order and economy. Learning about the biological structures and socio-political consequences of these viruses is the first step on that path."

"Thank you for your patience with my introductory 'sermon.' For next session, please watch Modules 1 and 3 of Kennedy's Virus Structures and Vectors series, which can be accessed in the SEP 101 materials file, located at National Online's info site. Or if you would like to access the chapters now, enter VC 'Kennedy 1 and 3,' and swipe your MedID across the IdentiPatch. Remember that this is restricted bandwidth/Level 3, so please download the modules to public space before viewing. 'Til next session…stay safe and healthy."

End file, intoned the MoniTV AVR. Sam sighed and entered VC "Off." The MoniTV instantly went blank. I guess I never realized how bad it was, she thought to herself. I've really been protected from most of it here. Maybe while I'm in school I'll join the Community Liaisons. I've heard MedRobotics needs a programmer. As Sam pondered her future, she went into the kitchen for her daily white cell count and a drink of Immunoboost.

THE ENEMY WITHIN

SUMMARY

Over the past 20 years, the U.S. has slowly, unexpectedly, but quite dramatically, unraveled. Like so many other nations at the height of their power, our pretensions, self-absorption, disagreements, ethnic tensions, and our single-issue politics have torn the social fabric. Our society is fractured and fragmented–politically, socially, and culturally. Intergenerational strife and separatists movements, compounded by high unemployment, have torn apart churches, neighborhoods, and families. Racial tensions are a tinderbox in both the cities and suburbs. Deaths from terrorist attacks no longer make the page one news. We have become the 'uncivil society.' And the worst part–the worst part for everyone–is the uncertainty. Violence can pop up at any time, and in the most unlikely places. We are caught up in vicious cycles of hate, revenge, and distrust. There seems to be no refuge. Under such social circumstances, capital and businesses are flowing out of the country. The nation's economy creaks along. Agriculture, health care and pharmaceuticals, low-end retail, personal security services, and construction are among the few bright spots. Government coalitions struggle to find an appropriate national response to the never-ending violence. All other national tasks and obligations are deemed unimportant, as the country faces the most critical turning point of its 250-year existence.

Seattle, Washington. April 12, 2021

The bomb destroyed the entire western wing of the U.S. Air National Guard building next to Seattle's SeaTac Airport. It exploded at midnight, long after the night cleaning crew was supposed to be gone. Three who worked late that night would never be going home. Three hours later a member of the response force finally noticed the note tacked to the wall. "We aim not to kill but to save. The wretched dictatorship of the U.S. government must be destroyed for all its citizens to be free." It was signed simply, "Northern Militia."

§

Later that morning, the Reverend Samuel Madison sat silently as the Domestic Protective Agency (DPA) helicopter touched down on the White House lawn and the sun began to rise. It had not been a pleasant ride – a lot of tension in the passenger compartment. The sergeant who was accompanying him had visited Madison's church before. That time he was running a scan for surveillance disruption systems. He stumbled on three Peoples' Rights militia members running out the back of the church. No one could prove that Madison knew they were there, but the sergeant knew. He knew that Rev. Madison was a traitor. He knew he gave solace to enemies of the nation. He couldn't understand why the President – the *President!* – treated him with respect.

Reverend Madison was glad to be on the ground. He had always hated flying, especially in these weapons-laden, noisy, vibrating machines. A friend had once described helicopters as "spare parts flying in formation." That seemed overly generous to him. He breathed a small prayer to himself when he felt the solid ground once again. President Esperanza had invited him to the White House on a number of occasions. As the pastor of the Truth Seekers Baptist Church, he had led executive prayer breakfasts a number of times before. This invitation was different. This was a personal plea from the President herself to help decipher the roots of the problems that plagued the country. Madison could hardly have declined.

The Reverend Madison had always had a unique insight into the national self-destruction that had become commonplace in the United States through his leadership in the Truth Seekers Baptist Church. The church had a progressive mission and a reputation for allowing citizens from any faction to worship in their cathedrals. The church also had a reputation for being safe from much of the electronic surveillance that pervaded daily life in the 2020s. The Reverend took pride in the open atmosphere he had created during his tenure there. It made it a place where uninhibited debate over the social issues challenging the country took place.

The Secret Service conferred with the DPA Team delivering him. A portable bioscan confirmed his identity, and the Reverend was hurried from the helicopter to the secure passage up past the Rose Greenhouse (the rising sun reflecting off the armor-glass). President Esperanza greeted him warmly in the Oval Office. Her expression of concern reminded him of the nature of the visit.

Without the usual media preparation, he noticed how tired she looked. She introduced him to the others seated with her — the Secretaries of Defense and the Interior, the Director of the Domestic Protective Agency, the Attorney General, the President's Chief of Staff and an entourage of policy advisors. The crowd looked as though they had been up all night. Madison was a bit overwhelmed by the gathering, and the President recognized this. "Sam," she said familiarly, "there was another attack last night. Three people died. I'm at wits end on what to do about …about this….this hell we are living. We need a new policy direction. You know the hearts of people of this country as well as anyone… and you understand the separatists better than anyone in this room does. Please, from your unique perspective, help *us* see things more clearly."

What she didn't tell Sam Madison was that the real reason they had been up most of the night had to do with international affairs. Those were issues with which she and her advisers had little experience and less expertise. Confirmed reports had just reached her that several months ago, both Europa and China had embarked on new and significant armament programs. The details were sketchy, but the sums being allocated appeared to be quite large. "It isn't enough," she thought, "that my own country is tearing itself apart in violence. The world is once again rearming. We must get our house in order!"

The request left him dumbfounded. He was about to ask why they would want him to evaluate a history they knew better than anyone. They undoubtedly knew things he did not – like his nagging uncertainty about the sources of the equipment, money, and intelligence that seemed to be at the hands of the separatists. But something stalled him from saying that. It was the look on the President's face; no, it was the haunted look in her eyes. A look shared by others around the room. His empathetic gifts did not desert him. These people, the leadership of the United States, needed help. They needed ministering. They were desperate. The society, the way of life and the rule of law they had sworn to protect and defend were on the verge of collapse.

He began as he almost always began. The Reverend Sam Madison sat down and smiled. It was a small smile at first; more of a sympathetic grin than anything else. But it grew. And as it grew, some of the tension came out of the room. He knew it would. It hardly ever failed. His smile was famous – in the streets of his community, in his church, in meetings with "separatists," even across the nation, thanks to the telenet. When he smiled, everyone agreed that he was the spitting image of jazz great Louie Armstrong. His smile could light up a room and make people's cares and worries fade into the background.

"Sam," said the President, " I know you have been writing a personalized history of the past twenty years. I've seen it. I'm sure it comes as no surprise to you, that everything you put on your computer is evaluated at the FBI. The fact that you occasionally minister to members of various separatist groups is an open secret and that makes you a full time surveillance target. I would like to say I am sorry, but, well…it's the times. I liked what I read, Sam. I learned some things from your perspective. I was hoping you would share those observations with my policy advisers."

"Actually, Madam President, I am not all that bothered by the surveillance. It is part of the social fabric of our time. So, be it. I *am* bothered, however, by the fact that it is an unfinished work – a very rough draft – that you have been reading. Frankly, I am a bit embarrassed, that's all."

"Yes, well, my speech writer tells me that you are having trouble choosing between third person 'objective' and first person 'subjective.' To be honest, that is what drew me to the narrative. Your text is a microcosm of the problem. Some things are objective fact. So much that is important, however, is subjective interpretation. I have taken the liberty of having the draft you were working on downloaded into my viewer. Could we discuss it together, please?"

Before he could answer, the DPA Director interrupted, "Madam President, before we…".

"Right, thanks for the reminder. Sam, the FBI discovered a sophisticated softbot planted in your system. They left it undisturbed, or at least they think they did. It is the kind of softbot they call a context correlator. It constantly searches your memory for contextually similar pieces of information and reports its conclusions as a rider on message traffic you generate. They tell me that this virus never works as well as advertised, but the one in your computer is among the best they have seen. We traced it when it went out with your morning mail. Our tracer got stripped off outside the U.S. Someone is reading your mail, Sam, and it's not just the good guys."

"Does that mean that the source of the softbot is a foreign power or that the message just takes detours before coming back into the U.S.?"

The President gave a quick glance at the DPA Director. He shook his head several times, as if telling her "no" to more than one thing.

"It could be either, Sam, ...but there's more to it." The DPA Director looked upset, but she went on anyway. "The FBI watched the softbot and discovered that it has a flag attached — a warning routine for other softbots. These other softbots are amazing. Apparently, your church accounts are being used to launder money. We don't know the source; not yet anyway. The money goes into your accounts, but for some reason, the bank's computers don't actually record an official deposit. However, when the money is pulled out and transferred, the sending and receiving banks 'see' the transaction as a legitimate withdrawal."

"Madam President, I don't know what to say. I never had any idea...I feel awful...what can I do. I'll close down the accounts immediately, of course."

"No, no, Sam. Leave things as they are. And, of course, I believe you. I know that you had nothing to do with this." The President had been watching the wall-mounted readout of her remote stress and lie detector system. It was showing green. She might like the guy, but you had to be careful. "Lets take a few moments for coffee and return to the reason for this visit."

As Reverend Madison sat down again, he saw that the first page of his text was up on a screen. The images flickered, as the viewer system adjusted phase-in with the counter-surveillance systems operating at the White House.

He wasn't sure how to begin, when he noticed that everyone had started reading. He decided to stay quite for awhile and see what emerged.

He began to read his own words with the rest of them. He noticed what the President meant. He did switch back and forth between first and third person. Oh well…

…however, as interesting as the 2000 Presidential elections were, they did not substantially impact the trends that followed.

At the turn of the millennium, the United States was at the apex of its global power exerting worldwide influence by political, economic and cultural means. Occasionally the U.S. employed militarily power, but did so with enough reluctance to make ourselves feel good about our intentions. Our long-term prosperity had given America the lowest poverty rate in history. Almost everyone in society benefited. Ironically, it may have been that very prosperity that brought the nation close to its demise.

Prosperity had an unanticipated consequence. With wealth and peace, came license and boredom. Even at the time, it was clear to many that prosperity created an unhealthy fixation on immediate self-gratification across many strata of U.S. society. We wanted what we wanted, and we wanted it now. Overwhelmed were our virtues of self-sacrifice, tolerance and civility. Many at the time called it the 'survival of the unfit.' Intellectual was "out." How "everyday people" lived and thought was "in." They made fun of the serious and sophisticated while demanding the indecent and raunchy. Public Television and "the Three Tenors" saw their best days in the mid 1990s. The likes of the World Wrestling Federation and Jerry Springer became icons of American culture.

I remember watching one of the defining moments in 2004. News stalwart Dan Rather was replaced by an anchor from Entertainment TV. The resulting "infotainment" quickly became the public's preferred news medium. Talk shows that rehashed violent or obscene subject matter dominated programming. Social critics called the phenomenon "the Springerization" of America.

Recreational drug use increased during those times; part of the self-gratification ethic. By the mid 2000s, drug use by people in all walks of life was unexceptional — so many people were on 24-hour highs (or lows). I remember the demands on my own father (the first Reverend Madison). A seemingly endless stream of families tried to cope with the addictions of loved ones. Hollywood picked up on this trend, producing several movies that became the clarion calls of the day — glorifying anti-authority themes, the freedom of the road, and the individualism of youth— all intertwined with the casual use of drugs. New methods of selling and distributing drugs hit the cities, suburbs and rural communities, including heavy use of the Internet.

"Reverend, this is all pretty old territory. The drug culture of the time was horrible and led to street and school violence. But, as the cause of today's problems – well that theory has been discredited."

"Actually Mr. Kline, I both agree and disagree. But let me say, first, that I am building an argument here. The drug issue is only the beginning. Everyone in this country has listened while one issue or another — more often, one group or another — has been labeled as *the* cause of our crisis. In fact, blame casting has actually become fuel for the fire. My thought is that the current crisis, at its roots, is not one-dimensional."

"I did not mean to get into this until later, but let me give you my bottom line assessment right now, before you read anymore. We have spent a decade and a half blaming one thing or another for our problems. It was the drugs. It was the Tech Bubble Recession. It was the cyber terrorists. It was the U.N. It was the Northern Range Militia. It was an after effect of high pollution levels. It was a conspiracy of Federal officials. It was the Sons of Liberty. On and on. The list of causes is almost endless. And for a decade the policies of the government and the polices of the separatists have been the same – to attack the one main cause, whatever they thought it was at the time."

"Well, let me give you another view. Do you all know how the early atomic reactors were built? They just piled up bricks of uranium until they had enough radioactive material to start a reaction. They built up layers until they got critical mass. No one layer was important by itself. It was only in the interaction of all the layers that things started to happen. To stop a reaction, you put in damper rods. You stopped the interaction from taking place."

"I see our current crisis using that analogy. Each issue in the last 15 years is a layer in the 'social reactor.' At some point, we got critical mass. The way to stop the problem is not by focusing on the layers, but by focusing on the interactions." He stopped talking at that point, thinking he had just made a fool of himself in front of policy experts. Everyone was looking at him in silence.
The President said, "Now you can see why I thought this might be a useful meeting."

Prosperity suffered a shock in 2006. Consumer confidence numbers had been falling for six months, and the market was jittery. Then several high tech firms reported out very disappointing earnings; enough to raise doubts about their financial viability. Most had been involved in various forms of e-commerce. A significant number of new offerings were introduced without high quality beta testing. Many of the new products failed for technological reasons. Others failed because the business models were flawed—elaborate e-business solutions for problems that companies or consumers did not recognize as important. In several cases, the new technologies had been introduced too soon on the heels of similar products.

These business failures across a critical industry came at a time of high price volatility within the market generally. It was a signal flag—the bull market was in trouble. Almost overnight, investment funds flew out of the high-growth technology stocks. In more extreme cases, their market capitalization fell by 75% in a few days. A significant number of highly leveraged, high-tech firms were unable to service their debt and collapsed.

The run on the high-tech stocks chilled the economy as a whole. Seeing paper wealth evaporate, consumers hunkered down and curbed spending. When the Fed worked hard to boost liquidity, a mild recovery ensued, but investors remained skittish about the high-tech sector and stayed with blue chips and "quality." After a few months, the "traditional economy" showed signs of some life. Falling interest rates helped encourage home and auto sales. In contrast, however, the high tech sector showed no signs of revival. Investors gave a cold shoulder to all new IPOs. *Business Week* said, "the market has returned to earth."

That had a chilling effect on the high-tech sector's hopes for recovery, leading to unemployment and disillusionment in that sector. It was predominantly made up of young, talented people who lost not only their jobs, but also their stock options. Their expectations of near-term wealth were shattered. They noted, however simplistically, that the big stodgy firms that employed the older generation did just fine.

These "techies" began to exact a very disturbing revenge. Within the next few months, there was a very notable trend on city streets, in malls, at ballgames, for the young to be rude and threatening to the middle-aged and elderly. They pushed and jostled when it was unnecessary. They spilled food and drinks and generally behaved "uncivilly" to all but their cohort. It was a behavior pattern that sprung up on the Internet; a suggestion by a few malcontents that spread like wildfire over the country. "Show the Geris that they can't have their way in everything." The incidents of young people in violent (self-righteous) exchanges with Baby Boomers became more and more common. I remember the nation's mood starting to turn nasty in that year.

Meanwhile, the mild recovery lasted no more than nine months. The problems in the U.S. high tech sector spread to Europe and Asia. Meanwhile the emerging markets found themselves on the losing end of the flight to quality and two Latin American countries fell into technical default on bond payments secured by the U.S. government. Currencies plummeted across Latin America and panic spread to Asia and Eastern Europe. A classic financial panic set in globally and demand fell across all sectors. Profound uncertainty fell over the global economy as bankruptcies skyrocketed and unemployment swelled.

With the destructive effects of the ensuing recession, recreational drug use swelled into an epidemic. Statistics dated 2007-08 indicated a use rate of 56% of high school and college age people and a rate of 41% in the ages 30-45. An increasingly well-organized criminal element now met new drug demand with new products, including a stunning array of harder narcotics and designer synthetic drugs.

Drug use and unemployment was now accompanied by a sharp increase in social violence, at this point sporadic, random, and differentially motivated. High schools and shopping malls became sites of mass killings resulting in over 150 dead in a dozen incidents. I was still in college then, and was horrified by what was happening. Malls were once havens where everyone felt at ease! It was then that I decided to follow my father and devote my life to healing that anger and disaffection. It seemed so simple then. Kids were misdirected and needed help — that was it.

The simmering resentment of the young high-tech workers expressed itself quite profoundly in 2008 through a series of devastating computer viruses. The third of the series was directed at the software division of the U.S. Center for Computer Research, and its effect became legendary. The virus named YUTES for Youths Under Totalitarian Executives Secede, hit every server in the division, destroying years of government study in artificial intelligence. Banks and financial institutions were subject to a barrage of viruses and intrusion attempts as well, each increasingly more sophisticated and disruptive. The effects on the economy were devastating.

"Dr. Madison, you do seem to be laying it on kind of thick about the role of the violent youth culture. This is part of your 'layering theme,' right?" The Secretary of Defense looked more puzzled, than argumentative.

"First, all of you, please call me Sam. Yes, I do tend to hit that rather hard. You're right. I lived through that time and was caught up in it a bit. I, too, had my anti-establishment period. But, as I look back, I think that the generational warfare that ensued really was a significant contributor. To carry on my analogy – it was two or three layers of the social reactor."

"The combination of the cyberchaos, drug usage, and violence created a groundswell of support for a law and order government. Candidates who ran against drugs and violence did well. Their victories did not have a calming effect, that's for sure, and the media only served to whip everyone into a greater frenzy over the divisive issues of the day. The generational breach became defined, not with political argument, but with mutually antagonistic behavior."

"I was in seminary back then, and still wince as I relive the heated arguments I had with my father over the 'unfairness' of Social Security, and his assertions that income disparity was 'a manipulated issue of a few malcontents, creating class and racial tensions.' My father was always wiser than I was, but back then I thought of him as politically unsophisticated."

"You know, now that you point it out, I probably am overdoing it a bit. I may have been using that section to work out some guilt that I still have over those arguments with my father."

The violence had really gotten out of hand, and the Federal government decided (after carefully reviewing polling data) that something drastic had to be done. The U.S. had to be de-weaponized. The President got gun control through Congress. The call to control all firearms was portrayed as an attempt to disarm U.S. citizens, creating a widespread backlash. An elaborate underground network for gun sellers emerged. The U.S. government responded with a new crime program: automatic felony status for carrying firearms across state lines, increase police recruitment, and mandatory sentences for "gun offenses."

The day after the President's announcement of his crime program all hell broke loose. Vigilante style shootings occurred in cities across the nation, killing dozens of people and causing serious rioting. Police in Denver refused orders to quell the violence, being hampered by insufficient equipment to respond to the well-armed rioters. As the rioting reached its peak, the Northern Range Militia entered Denver, notably uninvited, and within hours had restored order. The next day, however, as the Bureau of Alcohol, Tobacco, and Firearms (BATF) began its gun control program, a firefight broke out, as Northern Range Militia members refused to recognize BATF agents' jurisdiction in "their" city. Seven BATF agents and three militia members died.

The Denver tragedy started a long season of violence that spring. Clashes between police and militia or gang forces occurred sporadically nationwide. The Sons of Liberty got started in several states back then, with fairly persuasive literature. From the outset, they seemed to have links to the militia groups, yet preferred non-violent protests. As in the mountain states, forces in Michigan, Texas, Idaho, and Maine began to assume law enforcement roles in their communities, frequently clashing with local authorities. The most famous was the incident in Boise, Idaho on April 15, 2009. A confederation of the Mountain League militia and The Ethan Allen Corps infiltrated the Idaho State capitol and gained control of its buildings. Their message: the territory previously known as Idaho was now named the League of Mountain Unity and constituted its own sovereign nation. They invited all "foreign powers" out, giving twenty-four hours notice before considering their presence an act of war.

The President called out the National Guard, and their efforts to dislodge the militia lasted 21 days. It was a weird time in America, and I vividly remember some of my old high school friends rooting for the League like it was Notre Dame in the national championships. The stand-off, which had worldwide coverage and interest, concluded in the "heroic" deaths of 35 militia members as they detonated explosives and leveled the building. Their "martyrdom" was labeled an act "in defense of freedom." The hostage office workers suffered only minor injuries. The militia had placed them safely in the building's bomb shelter, an act that provided the dead with increased honor in the eyes of the world. Global sympathies were amazingly equally divided.

A national attitude of lost faith in the government's stewardship settled into all levels of the country. The two main political parties fractured, and what had previously been sub-groups now emerged as separate and credible political parties. First, the Jeffersonian Democrats and Lincoln Republicans emerged; later it was the Social Democrats and the Christian Republicans.

Most notable, however, was the emergence of new political parties — the YUTES and the Sons of Liberty.

Each stated their sympathies with many separatist groups, but vowed to work through political rather than violent means. While these new parties found most of their power at the state and local level, the traditional political system was altered fundamentally.

By this time, the drug culture had moderated, especially in the middle and affluent classes. As a fad, it had run its course. And state funded drug rehabilitation clinics at the community level were having a positive impact. That was the good news. The bad news was that a new addiction – hatred and violence – was taking its place.

The best and brightest began to leave the country for ex-pat jobs in Europe and Asia. The poor climate for research and development in the U.S. began a "brain drain" and many of the most talented found better work in other countries. And, it was not only individuals who chose to leave. In 2010, the United Nations announced its relocation to Brussels. Soon the Organization of American States moved to Brasilia. The U.S. remained in the North Atlantic Treaty, although the organization of NATO disbanded.

Despite the outflow of talent and institutions, Americans were inwardly focused. The election of 2012 was dominated by law and order issues and void of international emphasis. It was the first test of a U.S. political system involving not only two or three parties, but 10. We enjoyed the ability to align with narrowly defined parties, resulting in a highly fragmented, scattershot Congress — single issue politics at its most dramatic. Several factions backed a hard-nosed Presidential candidate unaffiliated with traditional political parties who promised to bring the rule of law back to the country.

The new administration's agenda was to re-establish law and order. It tried to beef up police forces to deal with the unrest and rampant crime, but after the Denver incident, it had difficulty recruiting. Equally so, recruitment for the National Guard was also difficult. Without adequate officers, lacking the sophisticated weapons of the curiously well-equipped gangs and militia, and needing to counter what he considered "the lies of the terrorist parties"; the Attorney General announced a program of heavily restrictive curfews.

Our economic growth, then, was flat,— maybe 1%— while the rest of the world began to climb out of recession in 2013. Congressional factions attempted to maintain trade relations, but given his narrow coalition platform, the President was loath to waste time on such issues. Anyway, the devaluation of the dollar helped U.S. goods stay competitive. Even so, U.S. corporations struggled to make a profit in that climate of crisis. Many moved key operations overseas. The business climate in Europe and South America provided a more reliable setting with skilled workers and a better infrastructure. Meanwhile, the Euro was becoming the dominant global currency.

On March 31, 2013, a major announcement was made regarding U.S. involvement in global affairs. In an effort to shift fiscal priorities, the President stated on worldwide telenet, that we would close many of our military bases abroad and recall our troops. As a result, and left unsaid, the U.S. power projection capability was to be barely maintained by a severely downsized Navy. An article in the *New York Times* quoted an unnamed White House source that confirmed that the reason for the troop withdrawal was to buttress internal law enforcement.

"Sam," said the President, "in the past I have heard you condemn this action as the 'last straw' from the perspective of the dissidents. Yet, in this text, you seem to downplay it a bit."

"Perhaps you're right Madam President. In many ways, I do believe this was a defining moment – the last layer to go on the reactor before critical mass. Do you remember what happened just after the announcement of the Army coming home? U.S. Marshalls arrested John Culver, leader of the Son's of Liberty and Amy Levy, Co-Chairperson of the YUTES. They were to have met with the Attorney General to discuss the implications of the troop movements. Instead, they were arrested with great fanfare on a bizarre technicality that won them a huge amount of public support. Especially, since it was clear that John Culver was roughed up a bit while in custody."

"I knew John back then, as now. He was a changed man after that incident. There was a kind of cold resignation in his manner. The tacit threat presented by the troop recall, mixed with the detainment and abuse was too much. He now had serious doubts that any compromise was possible. He and Amy began to side more openly with the separatists."

Early in 2014, the serious attacks began. Several explosions hit Washington, D.C. in the middle of the night of March 31, killing only five but establishing a gripping hold on the psyche of the nation. First was the bomb at the Herbert Hoover Building. Next were explosions that destroyed the FDR Memorial. Hours later, a third explosion occurred at the Bureau of Engraving and Printing. The final delivery that night was a simple grenade fired at the Old EOB, doing no significant damage but to the minds of the occupants. A message, without signature, was impaled on the White House fence: "We desire no deaths besides that of the police state. The U.S. government must go." A week later the President resigned and the Vice President stepped in.

In April, the FBI suffered repeated cyber attacks, virtually incapacitating its information systems. Random mutated computer viruses shot through the World Wide Web, too. Whether they were the unintended result of the cyber attacks or the work of some vicious little cyber-punks, no one really knew. The strangest turn of events back then was the emergence of a small group of cyber "White Knights" who would independently police the net and attempt to battle cyber terrorism. This type of vigilantism existed in the physical world as well.

In June, it got worse. Federal buildings in Boston, Houston, Phoenix, and San Francisco were simultaneously hit by missiles and mortars, leaving 754 dead and causing area rioting. During the response in each city, militia forces rose at the sites and opened fire on law enforcement and fire investigators, increasing the toll to 800. The average number of police and fire officer resignations the next day was 750 per state. Coordinated attacks by the militia groups, each with its national, internet-enabled network, became more prevalent over the next year. As a rule, targets tended to be economic infrastructure (bridges, rail, ports, cell phone towers, and so on.) and government installations (typically Federal, but occasionally state and local).

Unemployment was steady at 11%, and income disparity was becoming pronounced. The have's separated themselves from the have-not's. Gated communities gave way to walled communities, and owners did not hesitate to supplement law enforcement with private security forces. Security seemed to be inequitably dispersed for the benefit of the upper 15% of society, while the quality of life of the lower 85% suffered. For the first time, emigrtion exceeded immigration.

By mid-summer 2014, the new administration coalition was prepared to react decisively. On July 4, it implemented a program to use federal troops for domestic law enforcement, allowed forty-eight hour detainment of suspects, and suspended the Miranda Act. In an effort to demonstrate the political resolve of the administration, national security and domestic security organizations—and their respective intelligence organizations—were formally divided between two distinct agencies. The former operated as before under long-established rules, but with no gray-area domestic roles. The new super-agency operated with few prohibitions other than Congressional oversight (and that was *ex post facto*) for domestic surveillance or operations. Congress responded with deficit spending appropriations for increased pay and the acquisition of necessary equipment for law enforcement and intelligence programs. The new entity established to lead all internal security efforts was the Domestic Protective Agency. All domestic intelligence and law enforcement, including the U.S. Coast Guard, and excluding the FBI, was brought under its administration. From the outset, relations among the DPA, The FBI, and the CIA/NSA were complex and not especially cordial. Morale at the DOD was near zero. Suddenly, they had confusing, unorthodox, and unpopular missions, with inappropriate training and equipment.

The difference between the rhetoric of enforcement and the actuality of martial law, however, was something the citizenry was not prepared to see. Conditioned to witness

the bombing of empty office buildings and archaic stone
monuments by unidentified groups, people now recoiled
when officers of the law attacked warehouses being
used by separatists and terrorists. Prison crowding led
to abuse and disease The National Bureau of Corrections
received numerous rebukes from Red Cross inspectors
and Amnesty International representatives.

"I must tell you all," said the President, "that we have only just
confirmed that during that time a most devious attack was launched
on U.S. communities. We never knew it then. Someone poisoned
the grass, trees and bushes of thousands of community parks all
across the nation. It seems like a small thing, but it was devilishly
clever. It had a long-term lasting impression on people to watch
their beautiful parks slowly die off. In some ways, it was more
effective than a bomb—than a dozen bombs–on public morale.
We never knew it until now, because who keeps 'security' statistics
on parks? Who thinks of parks as targets?"

"We thought it was just our town," said Sam Madison. "You're
right, it was horribly depressing to watch our park wither. It was
like watching the country wither and die, which was the intent, I
suppose. That must have been the first example of the new forms
of attack we see today."

Recognizing their limitations in dealing with clandestine
groups that seemed to have significant financial resources
and weaponry, Domestic Protective Agency leaders
increased the monitoring of all of us. Even normal
citizens were monitored, and spent a part of their budget
to purchase defensive technology (sold in a vibrant black
market) to combat unwanted surveillance. Consumers

became sophisticated in their understanding of surveillance techniques and avoidance methods. The majority of the populace began to wonder if any side of the conflict was sane.

The vacuum left by the United States' withdrawal from foreign affairs was filled by regional powers in some areas, by criminal organizations in others (particularly the former Soviet Empire). The recently-coalesced Europa took center stage on most international matters, and was soon recognized as a primary world power. There were repeated clashes in Asia between China and its neighbors over disputed territory, but even Europa gave hardly a glance when China originally took Taiwan and later "helped" unify Korea. Brazil assumed an economic leadership role in the Americas as it finalized the American Free Trade Agreement in 2012. Unmediated disputes in the Middle East altered the political configuration of that region slightly, but nothing challenged the authority of the Greater Islamic Confederation that had formed. Its influence and power were not localized to that region, but instead grew from its natural global network.

Generally, the world was a moderately peaceful place in the early 2010s with only token U.S. presence. But that was not to last. The growth out of recession in most parts of the world was accomplished at the expense of income equality and equal access to wealth. Civil unrest began to emerge and was often brutally repressed. At the same time, ethnic disputes (some of ancient heritage) and old national rivalries began to resurface. This time disputes over water resources, territorial waters, and cross-border pollution were often the catalysts. While the U.S. wallowed in internal chaos, the world began to rearm. Within the U.N., two "voices" were to be heard. One asked if the U.S. could not be somehow brought back into the global political structure. The other voice (often spoken by new and asseryive regional powers) wanted no part of U.S. involvement.

The key manner by which foreign events impacted the U.S. was through the media. More and more, Americans seemed to be influenced by foreign news reports that focused on the old and new ethnic, religious, national, and racial offenses that Americans once thought they had left behind. Now they were re-introduced into the American political scene. Indeed one would read the articles and almost think that they had been deliberately engineered to inflame U.S. tensions.

The internal U.S. political fragmentation resulted in a marked rise in political activism. My church was awash in heated debate. Various parties challenged the suspension of domestic freedoms, while others called for greater controls. Many parties called for the U.S. to reestablish its former global role, while others called for the dissolution of the country. Parties demanded more privacy and the right to self-defense; still others fought for the registration of all citizens. The first ominous calls were heard for a second constitutional convention from vastly different interest groups with competing agendas.

These and other divisive matters reached a peak in the election campaign of 2016. A record number of candidates entered the field, resulting in a lot of confusion, and the campaign was marred by continuous violence. Early in the campaign, three candidates came to blows in a nationally televised debate. In September 2016, one candidate proposing citizen ID badges was shot and killed as he spoke in a Kentucky hotel; no other candidate picked up that platform.

The result in November 2016 was an administration led by the nation's first Hispanic President. Carolina Esperanza ran her campaign on a quiet platform of healing that demanded nothing and asked rather vaguely only for a return to the nation's common themes. Her message was that the separatists had gone too far *and* the Government had gone too far. At the time, I thought she didn't articulate any solutions and I couldn't support her, but she seemed to entrance many of my parishioners. By her inauguration in January in 2017, however, Esperanza had made some strides in opening the communication gap between embattled forces, slowing down the violence.

Immediately Esperanza negotiated an end to martial law, although she retained the authority and budgetary license to marshal forces should she see the need. She did retain the Domestic Protective Agency. I remained skeptical. The only elements that she cancelled, in fact, were the detainment period and Miranda allowances; all other martial law vehicles remained in place.

True to their word, leaders of the primary militia groups arranged for the cessation of their attacks. These leaders soon discovered, though, that it was much easier to build a coalition for action than it is to dismantle the same coalition in the name of inaction. Lower ranking militia members saw it another way, deriding the high politicking as demonstrations of their leadership's disconnect with the militia cause. They went their own way. Violence broke out in June.

Esperanza shifted her tactics. Recognizing the need for youth employment and infrastructure repair, Esperanza instituted a program second in size only to FDR's Civilian Conservation Corps. Initially created to repair physical infrastructure, she expanded the program to include the computer infrastructure that had been long neglected. Derided in the press as hiring the same people who had destroyed the bridges, buildings, and computers, she forged onward. When the conservative press criticized the congressional leaders who were funding the program, she was forced to cancel the effort. The effect again on my young flock was the same—promises terminated by rich adults.

Despite the fact that the economic outlook had improved somewhat and that the total number of violent incidents had declined, Esperanza still felt she had not found the right formula. Urban violence continued sporadically, occasionally marked by an intensity that made it impossible to distinguish good guys from bad. Cyber attacks continued against government facilities.

In the last nine months, the conflict has taken a new turn. The separatists have begun to use new and very creative tactics in reaction to the President's modestly successful anti-violence policies. Water systems in states and locales that support the President have had foul tasting chemicals added. Nothing lethal (yet), but the message was clear. Recently, a popular children's program had the content subtly shifted so that all of a sudden children all over the country were watching a pro-separatist story. The blending had been perfect. Within the last three months, many anti-separatist civic leaders across the U.S. have suddenly taken pro-separatist stands using almost identical language. Finally, businesses have noticed subtle mistakes in their corporate information systems. Instead of crashing systems, cyberterrorists have shifted to a much more cunning (and ultimately more devastating) form of attack.

It is my belief that our internal conflict has reach a new, more socially destructive, stage. Bombs will undoubtedly still be used, but far more clever and subtle forms of attack are now being employed.

So, where are we now? The militant separatist groups have done enormous physical, psychological and cultural damage to the country for over a decade. They continue to propagate their mayhem with considerable effectiveness. Yet, I think they have lost some of their legitimacy in the eyes of the American public. Thanks to the new President, the middle of the American political landscape seems to be returning to its senses. But, it is so complicated! Hate has become a way of life for so many that trust is very hard to find. The Sons of Liberty and other political parties must be brought into the system. Yet they have much to fear based on past U.S. Government behavior and are rightfully skeptical. There is then this new form of attack.

"Well, I had hoped to see what your advice might be. How do we bring sanity back to the U.S.?" said the President.

"With all due respect, Madam President, that kind of depends on the people in this room."

"Well certainly there is truth in that, but I think you may have named your own poison, Sam. I think some of the solution may well depend on you. First, I really think you are on to something when you focus on breaking up the interactions among the layers, as you put it earlier. Second, you are right about the inconsistency between dwindling support for the separatists and the continuing efficacy of their war on our society. Third, we do need some constructive engagement with the Sons of Liberty. Fourth, we all know that you are unique. You are respected by many on all sides of our uncivil society. You are the only person I know who can speak with John Culver, Amy Levy, and others, as well as Carrie Esperanza."

A moment of silence…."I will not become your political agent, Madam President."

"Were you to do that, you would lose your ability to bring peace to our nation. And you know something, Sam? I think we just might be able to do it." With that, the President got up and walked over to her desk. She brought back a simply carved ivory letter opener. "Thomas Jefferson used this when he was President. I would like you to deliver it into the hands of John Culver. Just a small gift; no message – except maybe to say that, if he were to use it to open a letter from the White House, I would be well pleased."

§

Later that night The President was on a flight to Texas to visit her mother. She had some hope in her heart, although it was tempered by years frustration and anguish. However, Sam Madison's analysis had her focusing far more than she used to on questions of funding and communication among all the disparate anti-government groups. She wondered if there was not some carefully orchestrated foreign involvement in our domestic problems. Many of her people in the National Security apparatus had been saying that for years, but she always discounted it. She paid more attention to the DPA, and they did not believe it. Budgetary politics, or is the DPA right?

She had seen movements to counter the violence and hatred domestically, and a reduction in popular support for many radical causes, yet the violence continued. And the separatist groups seemed as well funded as ever. And these damnable new forms of attack! That was not the work of the militia people she had ever met.

Yet, she had hope. The Reverend Madison gave her hope and her phone conversation with her mother gave her hope. Her mother had told her what a difference she would see during the next few days. "There is less gang violence and better relations between police and militia," her mother explained. "Folks had gotten together to chat about things, they'd gotten so bad. And we all figured we had to stick together. We started this group, and we meet and talk things over, let each other know what's going on. Hell, I even help some of them kids out when they need some cash, and they help me out with the farm. A similar group just got started in the next town."

She was thinking about community involvement, and escalating violence, and foreign involvement, and her mother's rice pudding, when her aide handed her a message form. By the look in his eyes, she thought, it must be another bombing.

> XXO77932/authentication443b2/ToPOTUS/textbegins:
> Eyewitness reports the following events. On the flight back
> to Virginia, the Reverend Samuel Madison was making
> conversation with the sergeant who had picked him up.
> Reverend Madison pulled out the letter opener to show
> the sergeant. The sergeant shot reverend Madison through
> the heart. The sergeant explained that the secret service

MILITANT SHANGRI-LA

SUMMARY

Militant Shangri-la is a frightening world of unexpected events and difficult-to-trace villains. The world in general, and the U.S. in particular, has continued into a third decade of a prosperous, information-driven economy. But the world is also continuing along the road to Complexity, with new structures of influence on the globe—some which hardly could have been imagined in the 1990s. The Newtonian diplomatic and military calculus of the past 400 years since nation states arose closing the Middle Ages seems to be giving way in turn to another New Age. In particular, the global man-in-the-street has endured a past century of 200 million deaths in war, dizzying and difficult technological change, and is listening sympathetically to the very Earth groan under the burden of pollution and extinction. Mankind needs hope, and most men are ready to receive it.

Into this world there now comes a worrisome Alliance. South Africa, India, Indonesia, China and others–all pariahs to the West where individual liberty and human rights are still the enduring social philosophy–have come together in a multidimensional cartel. The U.S., its four English-speaking cousins, and their Pacific allies Japan and a now-unified Korea are both determined and assertive in their global involvement. They view the Alliance as they have past threats, as a new bloc of nations, another evil empire of the ilk they have seen before.

But things are never what they seem in a complex world. Political, military, and economic actions yield unpredictable reactions in dimensions of policy—as the West was to learn in the decade from 2010-2020 when the Alliance was teaching it new tricks. For the Alliance operated both *legitimately* as a block of aligned nation-states and *illegitimately* as criminal cartels, and the twain often met. What was good for business was good.

For the first time since the rise of the British Empire, the Alliance had created a genuinely effective Grand Strategy. It would keep the world on the edge of chaos; simply that and no more. And from that chaos—it would profit, never letting the Americans and their allies settle the world down into a single "balance of power." It was enough to make Henry Kissinger roll over in his grave. More, the Alliance saw with clarity what the West's bureaucratic governments refused to see: there were now no longer "spheres of influence" so familiar to Whitehall and Foggy Bottom. Now, the means for multiple planes of influence – new instruments of power, involving global media, new weapons, and profitable criminal enterprises–had arisen. The Alliance was in space, on the seas, in the media and working into the hearts and minds of the world to kill the idea of personal liberty. With religion, nationalism, ethnicism, media, philosophy, art, music, the Alliance was harnessing the New Age yearning of the common man for its own use. One for all–and all for the Alliance. To the dismay of the West, many a man was ready to be domesticated.

Future History: The Road to 2020
Introduction

From the 20th floor of Bank of Oceana building in Taipei, Tzu Mai Lei gazed out over the South China Sea toward the mainland, so long the direction of danger. Now, nearly 60 years after Taiwan separated from China, resolution of the long conflict between the two Chinese cultures had appeared at last on that distant horizon. No one would have believed it would have come out this way, Tzu thought to herself. There are indeed new things under the sun.

Behind her she heard the clink of glasses and ice. Padwanna Sukarno offered her a glass of champagne and smiled. "To business."

Her grandfather, she knew, would have been proud of her. Tzu was the eldest daughter of one of the great families of Chinese expatriates with business dealings all over the Pacific Rim, from Santiago to Sakhalin Island. Shipping, banking, real estate, and construction concerns were at the heart of the Tzu family empire. They were respected around the world. More–much more–they were feared. For the other side of the family business was crime– less visible, but *very* organized and *very* profitable, crime. Drugs, money laundering, extortion, murder, mercenary force, piracy— whatever was profitable. Mei Lei's ancestors had been in both "businesses," the black and white worlds, for generations.

To the Tzu, the line between crime and business was a fool's illusion, and the family refused to be fools. Most of us speak truthfully not because we believe the people to whom we are speaking are honest, but because we believe it right to be truthful, it is an act of individual ethics, an individual choice.

For the Tzu, ethics were less useful than tactics. "We deal honorably with our friends and treacherously with all others," her grandfather had taught her. And it had stuck. Mei Lei had learned well. Now, as the "Godmother" of the Taiwanese crime families, Tzu Mei Lei had truly changed the world. With her Indonesian partners, they had created a whole new kind of global power – an amalgam of nation states, religions, ethnic groups, corporations, and crime. First one face, then another, and another, and another still.

The truly remarkable thing, she thought to herself as she took a sip of her champagne and clicked on the television, was that her enemies in the West didn't even know she existed. To them, the "Alliance," as the West called it, was a worrisome confederation of pariah states. First South Africa and India in 2003, then Indonesia a year later, China in 2010, and now, amazingly, the admission of Taiwan. Taiwan in bed with China! To the U.S. State Department, still living in the Newtonian world of nation-state, the whole thing was impossibly complex. More, the growing geography of the Alliance was alarming. The Alliance could influence – possibly even close – some of the most important sea-lanes in the world. And that, smiled Mei Lei, wasn't the half of it. Mei Lei knew that Indian information and space technology, new highly advanced Chinese weapons, and a brilliant doctrinal approach to war in this New Age posed a real and formidable challenge at last to U.S. military power.

Let them come into the Indian Ocean or the South China Sea, and things will be different, she thought, knowing full well that using their new military power was not good for business. Far better that the Americans and the English just know....

Six thousand miles to the south, the Australian cabinet, meeting in extraordinary session, was decidedly less exuberant. For the last 20 years, Canberra had been watching Indonesia and her unlikely allies South Africa, India and China with growing alarm. Now, in January 2020 with the onset of southern summer, an especially cold and hard reality had set in. The "Alliance," as the northern partnership called itself, had announced the addition of Taiwan as the fifth member of the rogue group, creating a vast economic, political, and cultural cartel from the Cape of Good Hope to the Japanese Ryukus. The Australian Prime Minister, James Timothy (Timmy) McLeod was particularly disturbed that none of the intelligence agencies in any of the English-speaking nations – the five cousins – had had even a whisper of the Taiwanese move.

"It's like the Soviet collapse 30 years ago," he ranted at the eight members of the cabinet staring back at him. "How in the hell does it happen that we crash one empire and grow another – all in front of our very eyes and I get to watch it on television first? Taiwan? Taiwan? Taiwan joins China? What is that all about? It's a damn good thing you guys aren't in the media business. You'd starve to death. You get beaten to every story."

McLeod reached into the wooden box on his desk, took out a piece of paper and waved it disgustedly across at the adjacent table where the eight cabinet members sat, enduring yet another of the Prime Minister's profane tirades, so increasingly common these past months. His portly figure, cigar smoking, belligerence, and fondness for liquor had bought him the inevitable comparisons with Winston Churchill during the most recent political campaigns. It was a distinction he did not try to dissuade, finding it appealing to the voters.

"Do you know what this is?" he demanded, puffing on a huge cigar. "This is a request from the government of Singapore for an AUSCANZUKUS base to be built on the island. 'Surrounded' is the term they use. 'Surrounded.' What is this, 1941? What next, the Japanese Imperial Army on bleedin' bicycles?" Since the 1990's, both Australia and New Zealand had sat out the global good times. Economically, both countries had progressed little beyond the agricultural and tourist base that had sustained them since their colonial founding. An ill-fated attempt to create a software and information-systems industry had failed in the early 2000s under enormous competition by the Indian Bangalore companies. At the turn of the century, the Indian software industry was growing at 40 percent per year on sales of $1.2 billion. Five years later, it was skyrocketing at 700 percent per year and hadn't stopped since. More, Bangalore was possessed of seemingly endless financial resources – exactly from where, no one could ever figure out with any precision. Another flipping mystery, McLeod bitterly complained to himself.

McLeod knew what they all knew: there was little choice but to heed the Singaporean request for a presence. The Alliance – with cheap labor, seemingly endless money, an incredible space program that routinely launched one high-technology space vehicle after another, and now the economic clout of Taiwan – would sooner or later strangle the southern cousins.

And so Timmy McLeod struck his best Churchillian pose, blew out a huge cloud of smoke—unmistakably in the direction of the Cabinet—and said,

"Well, gentlemen, there's but one thing to do. We'll bring the Americans in—if we have to bloody bomb bloody Pearl Harbor ourselves again to do it. How we got into this mess, I'll be damned if I bloody know."

2000-2010

Padwanna Sukarno knew exactly. Possessed of a less lengthy pedigree than Tzu Mei Lei, his was no less sinister. As a distant and poor cousin in the powerful family that founded Indonesia in the 1960's, he had been forced to exercise his ambition behind the scenes. Like all the Sukarnos, he had been given a piece of the Indonesian revolutionary pie, though it was more like a sliver to his mind. But he would parlay his stake. A regional manager in the Bornese oil fields for the family, Padwanna developed the skills of a roustabout for survival, marrying them to an extraordinary intellect.

Such men are dangerous enough, but in this man there was also the added element of opportunism. And the world was full of opportunities. Padwanna believed that Great Men changed the world, and he knew he was such a man. Like Napoleon and

Alexander, endless audacity was his watchword. By the 1970s, despite the overthrow of his family years before by a new ruling dynasty, the Suhartos—Padwanna had burrowed himself deep within the labyrinthine banking system of Indonesia, which supported more than 300 private and 90 state banks in those years. Among them was Padwanna's Bank of Oceana, which by 1979 had grown to be 10th in size in the country with 780 branches across the archipelago.

Money from the U.S.-Vietnam rout in the 1970s, from the Burmese transition to Myanmar, distantly from the rise of the Medellín cartels in Colombia, and from a hundred other events poured into the Bank of Oceana's coffers. With it came the inevitable long lists of favors and contacts, each duly recorded in Padwanna's private books. There were lists of Indonesian military officers, wealthy from the rewards of Suharto's policy of regionalization in the 1980s. These officers, many of them peasant boys cut from the same cloth as Padwanna himself, made it profitable to do business on an individual and regional level across the islands. There were lists of others, including a number of offshore banking connections that kept Suharto money safe in troubled time.

Above all, there were lists of Chinese, the largest ethnic minority in Indonesia. In the late 1960s after the overthrow of Padwanna's Sukarno cousins, the Chinese began to prosper, nurtured by the now-reigning Suharto family. So powerful and wealthy did they grow that the Javanese used a new title for them—the Cukong, Chinese for "master" or "lord." The Cukong became the masters of capital. The Indonesian military, the masters of politics. The Bank of Oceana became banker to both, moving huge sums of money in and offshore, ever expanding both its legitimate and illegitimate ties. When the Indonesia fell into revolution in 1999, Padwanna helped his Chinese customers carry more than $80 billion off the islands–always, of course, remaining in Bank of Oceana accounts.

Four years later, when the slowly recovering Indonesia stumbled once again into financial crisis, the International Monetary Fund was unwilling to help, stretched thin for resources and lacking a consensus for an Asian financial solution. For Padwanna Sukarno, it was a Napoleonic opportunity. Within a month of the crisis, Sukarno had arranged for an independent banking solution, bringing both the Chinese accounts and the Chinese back to Indonesia. In the 2003 elections, the first Indonesian president of Chinese extraction was elected. Padwanna had bought himself a country.

It was about that time that Nelson Mandela died, a victim of age and a broken heart. Africa, poor Africa, had been beaten to its knees by colonialism, by corruption, by tribalism, by hunger, by plague. South Africa was once more hated in the world. In the face of a continental-wide plague that affected millions in sub-Saharan Africa, South Africa shut its border down with a resounding clang not heard since the Berlin Wall. Night after night, the world reeled in shock by news images of South Africans–black and white alike–beating, looting, and shooting the hundreds of thousands starving and plague-ridden refugees encamped on their northern border. Even to a world already steeled by decades of cruelty on television, the sheer brutality of the South Africans was incredible to watch.

By the time Mandela closed his eyes at last, Africa was transformed, not into the bright vision that he and others had hoped and helped to convey, but into a tribal morass of bestial cruelty where the vestiges of nations and states remained only on maps and globes. South Africa itself, the last bastion of European culture, was determined at any cost not to follow the rest of the continent into chaos.

In the U.S., the political pressure applied by African-Americans in reaction to the South African policies only strengthened the willingness of the government and the rest of the outraged citizenry to act.

Act it did, laying down a different kind of Iron Curtain around South Africa. This time, an absolute trade barrier to which most of the world and all of Europe and North America subscribed. U.S. consideration of a naval blockade to boot was leaked out to the media as trial political balloon, all part of a Western policy to pour the milk of human kindness down throat of Pretoria. The South African response startled not only television viewers around the world, but also of the U.S., the United Nations, NATO and most of the rest of the established political world. Within four days of the U.S.-planted threat in the media, the television once more showed images of South Africa—this time of the Indian fleet arriving off Cape Town. Within two more days, elements of the Indian air force and army arrived for billeting in nearby Simon Town, the principal South African port. And, on the seventh day, the two nations announced a formal mutual defense and economic treaty. Within a month, U.S. intelligence agencies got their first look at the Indian Navy and Air Force acting in evident professional skill in a series of sea control exercises in the Indian Ocean. Long-range sensors, sophisticated communications, and some surprising new weapons were deliberately showcased to demonstrate to the U.S. that they were not the only military power in the world that had learned the Revolution in Military Affairs.

What the South Africans got out of the deal was protection; what the Indians got was respect – and strategic geography. Since 1998, the Indian body politic had been in turmoil, with but two enduring policies—military buildup in the face of Pakistan and the development of an information technology industry base. By the time of the South African crisis, they had achieved both. The U.S. intelligence community had discovered an Indian ballistic missile "gassed up and on the pad" a year before during the height of yet another Indo-Pakistani round of brinkmanship. The image was released to the world media, with the net result that India became both a world pariah and a world power. The deal with South Africa now threatened, for the first time since the Portuguese explorations five hundred years before, to return the Indian Ocean to Indian hands.

2010-2020

Horrible that it was, all this played in the background of the everyday world. For Europeans and Americans, enjoying still the economic fruits of the Information Age, India and the Indian Ocean was a long way off. And, in Des Moines, congregations of good people prayed for Africa, but it was, after all, Africa. The American GDP was growing at 4.5 percent, still selling into a global marketplace. Inflation was under control and predictable.

Those who had the education, and most did in America (and in Europe), could work. The recognized need for education in a high-technology world had spurred a spectacular growth in Internet-based education. Elementary school children and post-graduate students alike went to school on the net. The merger of television, computers, and entertainment made learning a powerful experience, which did not escape the attention of the Sunday *New York Times* pundits who viewed the potential for "propaganda" with alarm. But the Internet was alluring, paving the way for a large new industry of "voucher" schools, and the combination of the two returned (some) children to prayer in the hundreds of private schools that had popped up. Like abortion and gun control, prayer in schools was one of those perennial issues on the American political agenda. No one wanted to play catch with that one again, and so schools in America and in much of the world became seductive, fractious, and an extremely powerful in shaping public opinion in the long term. Non-public schools, once the domain of religious groups, now became full-fledged non-governmental organizations, teaching children all manner of reading, writing and rhetoric.

The move to "wired" schools came with a series of remarkable twists. In 2010, the long-nationalized British Broadcasting Corporation transformed itself into a global medium exporting British cultural and ideas—all in search of considerable profit. The new BBC offered education and degrees with prestigious British university backing, put forth the British point of view on civilization, and reported the world news.

Its rival system, ***Earth*TM**, began operations in the same year, combining themes of environmental awareness, a new spiritualism, and global brotherhood–usually accompanied with a persuasive dose of degradation for rapacious capitalism, the perpetual and pathetic struggles of the have-nots, and the groaning of Mother Earth. The BBC was drowned out.

By 2015, *Earth*™ had emerged as a strikingly new source of world power – an "electronic religion," the *Sunday Times* graybeards called it. "Biased Only Toward The Planet" was on the masthead of every net screen, and its spinning green globe logo was a welcome presence around the world reminding all of its cornerstones: "credible news, affordable education, human respect." *Earth*™ had a seemingly endless supply of money for scholarships and flashed on the screen thousands of success stories of those it had helped into the New Age. Money flowed into *Earth*™ banks and commercial enterprises. Money flowed out of *Earth*™ in the form of loans and grants. In 2014, *Earth*™ raised $50 billion from global "contributions" and, in a global, mediacast rock concert, 70-year-old Sir Elton John handed over the check to Amazon tribesmen representing the Brazilian government for rainforest relief. To many, *Earth*™ seemed to reflect all the good in the human spirit and showed what could be done when consensus and partnership reigned in the local and global villages.

And that was music to its bankers' ears, principal among them and sitting amidst the many world dignitaries seated to the right of the tribesmen was the beaming Padwanna Suharto. Sitting next to him was Lao Jai Sheng, Premier of China.

Within a month of the concert, China, India, South Africa, and "greater Indonesia" – the last an informal name for the set of

Alliance-friendly Southeast Asian nations from Myanmar to Papua – entered into the formal treaty known to its members as *"Constellation of Southern Stars"* and, more simply, as "the Alliance" to the West. Its new flag – gold stars on a green background – conveyed a vision of a new world future.

Along with the rest of the world media, *Earth*™ mediacast the formal signing of the treaty, but exclusively covered the rest of the story. Two more explosions occurred.

First, the Alliance announced that its member nations had been in technical cooperation for a decade before joining together to construct a huge new space station and that they would launch its already constructed components in rapid sequence during the coming year.

The second shoe to drop was its purpose. The Alliance countries, long the principal polluters of the world, announced they had collectively seen the light, as the Indian Premier's announcement sound bite characterized it. The Alliance and *Earth*™ would work together to clean up the world. *Earth*™ would guarantee the Alliance's commitment, and GAEA would provide the data for the world to see. Though the space station had been designed in secret for military purposes, Premier Lao smiled into the camera next to his Indian colleague,

"Now it is for plowshares."

Now also the pace was picked up. *Earth*™, with its attentiveness to philanthropy (and, Western pundits said, to public relations)

became a huge vehicle for commerce. Dollars that went into *Earth*™ were plowed back into people and the Earth itself—creating a huge new marketplace. In 2017 *Earth*™ opened the first global stock market, online. All the while, Padwanna and his always increasing list of partners grew wealthy. In 2018, Padwanna Sukarno was named one of the 10 wealthiest men in the world, as the Bank of Oceana announced a partnership with the new international *Bank of Earth*™.

That same year, the Dean of the University of the Southern Constellation was awarded the Nobel Peace prize for his *Manifesto for a New World,* in which he called for humans to hold out hands to help each other by disdaining the violence and emptiness of Western culture. He viewed with alarm a growing amount of criminal activity in the world, from plain old piracy to Information Warfare. He applauded the efforts of the Alliance in fighting against the rot of the past 400 years of the "Western" Age. The Alliance, he said, was the "new dawn in the East for the New World."

Strange things happened, as they always do in any world. Several major banks in Switzerland failed amid the rumors of fraud. A U.S. reconnaissance satellite was destroyed in an apparent collision with space junk. India, with its movie and information technology industries, was giving California a very hard run in its role as the "Eastern Hollywood." The African plague was left to run its course – to the surprise and despair of every optimist in the world. Millions died, but the Alliance and its member South Africa were ready to invest in a new Africa to replace it. In 2019, China announced its especial concern for expatriate Chinese all over the world, but most especially in the Western Hemisphere, where it saw prejudice against Asians as manifest. Alliance diplomats became frequent flyers to Latin America, where many of the Alliance-**Earth**™ philanthropic dollars were being spent.

In a startling move very late in 2019, all the nations of the Alliance announced an Afro-Asian transport tax, wherein all goods and services moved into their area of interest were taxed. To the West, and to the small, surrounded city state of Singapore, this move was intolerable – especially in view of numerous incidents at sea and mysterious sinkings of non-Alliance shipping.

And, for no apparent reason, the Olympic Committee announced that the 2024 games would be held in Tibet.

End State: 2020

"I think this is it," Padwanna said, pacing in his Jakarta Bank of Oceana office as the images came onto the screen. On the screen, above the **Earth**™ logo, the Dalai Lama smiled serenely at the global audience.

"My friends," he said slowly and with emotion, evoking in many viewing images of Mahatma Gandhi.
"Today I am profoundly honored–and very grateful–to tell you of the return of our ancient homeland of Tibet to the Tibetan people. It has been a long wait and an arduous journey to freedom. I mean this not just for Tibetans, but also for all of us in this troubled world. For hundreds of years our lives have been ruined by greed– the tyranny of capitalism. ...By war, the tyranny of fear. ...By hate, the tyranny of ego.

"Over the past decade, a new force for a greater good has emerged. It has taken us over one and all, restoring to our race the vision of a future of human respect. Killing greed. Killing ego that enslaves us to ideas of individualism and a material life. It is a swelling in the soul of the globe. The so-called Enlightenment of 300 years ago – the fundamental belief in selfish personal life, selfish personal liberty and, above all, the greed of personal pursuit of happiness – brought the human race in the end to near extinction and has nearly destroyed the planet itself."

"I tell you tonight," his beautiful face lit up as he spoke, "There is new hope for all of us – not just some of us. A second, a real Enlightenment is underway. I, and the people of Tibet, express our profound thanks for Premier Lao for the return of our land and our profound respect for his wisdom and leadership…" .

Those sitting around the table behind him watched as Padwanna's shoulders rose and fell into a deep sigh. After a slight pause, he snapped off the screen and turned to face his partners, men and women from all over the world, with a broad smile. Abruptly, his facial muscles hardened into its more familiar posture of total concentration and intensity.

"We must watch this thing in Singapore that it doesn't get out of hand, " he said. "Manage it. Keep it always on the edge. …Always on the edge–never over it."

A few hundred miles away across the Malaccan Straits, the Raffles Hotel in Singapore was a seedy museum of old furniture covered in old dust. Even its famous Singapore "Slings" were old-fashioned. In a world of instant personal communicators, global trade, and

Earth™, Raffles was right out of the films—the British films. Yet, it carried with it a symbolism to those seated around the huge briefing complex, which had been hastily constructed from one of the hotel's large and ornate ballrooms. They were not going to lose the city *again*—and certainly not to another Greater East Asia Co-Prosperity Sphere.

Swinging at anchor at Singapore roads a few miles away, were USS Roosevelt and her brand new Royal Navy sister, HMS Churchill, the first British carrier since the 1968 decision to kill British big decks 50 years before. Surrounding the hotel were soldiers and marines from the U.S., the U.K., Canada, Australia and New Zealand—the "cousins" in battle dress. The whole scene was reminiscent of a World War II conference – some surreal modern day Casablanca, Yalta or Cairo.

The indefatigable Timmy McLeod was just finishing a long litany of suspicions about the Alliance. They were the conspiracy behind the occasional, but nearly catastrophic disruption of global communications. It was the Alliance, he said, that was conducting Information Warfare, dallying here and there in this bank and that. It was the Alliance, with all its sickening drivel on **Earth™** all the time that was eroding the legacy of 300 generations of Western Civilization. On and on he spoke, without interruption from anyone, though he was politically the most junior of the statesmen present.

Finally, after nearly two hours, Admiral Turner Jones, Commander of U.S. Forces Pacific, rose to give the American military position.

"Prime Minister," he began slowly, walking through the tables to the huge chart of the Pacific and Indian Oceans on the wall. Pausing for a moment to take a deep drag on his 40th or so cigarette of that day, the tall Admiral in the immaculate white tropical uniform then shifted his gaze straight on at McLeod and began with a sigh,

"All this is likely true," Mr. Prime Minister. "I do not doubt it. But, what is it, precisely, you wish? Together, we five cousins and our allies," he nodded to the Japanese and Korean officers seated near his own staff, "have assembled a combined fleet smaller than any time in our history. Powerful, to be sure, but small. Nor is it different with the combined armies. We have together less than 30 divisions.

"And," he flipped through an index card in his other hand, "as of this morning, six operational air wings. Against that, we are faced also with a less formidable force than past wars have seen in these waters. The Alliance's forces are no better than ours, but not much worse. They are backed by first-rate intelligence and high technology weapons, just as ours are. I have no doubt that we could have one hell of a bunch of battles here.

"But," he said, sweeping his cigarette hand across the expanse of Southern Asian waters, smoke drifting from South Africa to Taiwan. "But, I have grave doubts we could have a war.

"I, for one, am not willing to turn the clock back to global nuclear war–and I don't think you are either. I can't hold the whole Indian and Pacific Oceans with naval power while 30 divisions take on one-half of the planet's geography." The Admiral then walked the room across the Eastern Hemisphere in a 50-minute expert tour of military strategy and the limits in general of military power in dealing with the Alliance.

"All of this points to two conclusions in my mind. First is, that any military action we *can* take will be unsustainable in this theater. Second, that the Alliance took to heart the lesson we should have been learning lo these many years,

"Power, like wealth, is simply different in the 21st Century."

McLeod took a heavy draw on his cigar and, sitting down, poured water into his glass and stared long into the silence of the room.

NEW CAMELOT

SUMMARY

These are good times for the U.S., and good times for most of the world. We enjoy economic growth, international stability, technological progress and the fruits of an energy breakthrough that promises cheap fuel and a clean environment. Most American citizens sleep soundly without worries of global conflicts, physical threat or financial insecurity. Large, horizontally integrated global corporations drive strong consumer markets and keep products, services, ideas, and technology flowing across borders. The global economy churns with machine-like efficiency. The U.S. no longer dominates militarily and economically, but at a time of rising affluence and an ever-improving quality of life, who cares? The U.S. is still very involved and assertive in world affairs. For the first time in anyone's memory, the past is not recalled wistfully. A confluence of factors got us here—globalization, governmental reform, information technology, among them—and promise to sustain our forward progress. But there are, of course, no guarantees. Not all the world is sharing equally in these good times; some nations are left out, perhaps too far behind in skills and infrastructure to play in this very competitive, free, and global marketplace. But the mood is bright, government is visionary, firms are dynamic and we all believe in the future.

"Foundations of Our Common Future": A Symposium

Editor's note: These transcripts have been edited for length, but not for content.

Welcome and Introduction

By Andrea Acevedo MacNeil

Ladies and gentlemen, welcome to part one of the sixth annual Global Issues Symposium. This year's event is entitled "Foundations of Our Common Future" and is sponsored by the Starbucks Foundation, in collaboration with the United Nations Science Technology and Development Organization and Global Space Ventures, Inc. Today I am pleased to present three outstanding global citizens, each of whom will examine major influences on the development of the modern age. To provide the broadest insights, we have selected experts who, together, can deal with the wide range of issues related to politics, public policy, technology, and international affairs. Each panelist will deliver a short presentation or speech, followed by one or two questions from the audience. I will begin by introducing Dr. Miriam Davis....

"The End of Government (As We Knew It)"

By Miriam J. Davis

Dr. Davis is author of *The Unexpected Renaissance: American Leadership in the New Century* (Microsoft & Harper Row Press, 2018) and Chief of the Office of Corporate Economics and Public Policy of the IBM Corporation in Armonk, New York.

I am pleased to be here with you today and to have this opportunity to kick off the symposium. I believe it is fitting that the lead speaker is a public policy specialist, because I feel strongly that any understanding of the changes that have swept through our society must begin with the profound changes in the role of the state over the last 20 years.

My first observation is simply that the world has turned out to be a lot stronger, healthier and safer than I expected it would be way back on the eve of the new millennium. Before you start bombarding me with examples of exceptions, which I do not deny exist, let me ask those of you old enough to remember back to the turn of the century: Did you ever think that we as Americans would enjoy largely uninterrupted economic growth and stability? That we would be spared major global conflicts? And that most of the rest of the world would benefit from prosperity and peace as well? It is hard to get proper perspective on our current state of affairs. But it is clear, and I think you will all agree, that in a decade or two we will look back on these times as extraordinary ones. In this sense, we are privileged to be participants in, and beneficiaries of, what I call the Unexpected American Renaissance.

Today, I will share my observations of the changes in government and public policy. For what it is worth, these are from the perspective of a senior officer of a large, global company. Time will permit me to touch on only a limited number of themes. I have chosen three that I think are among the most important.

1. Devolution Delivered

I argue our extraordinary living standards and high quality of life would not have taken place without fundamental changes in the relationship between the government and American society. The miracle of the American democracy is dynamic change, which sometimes is painful and unclear in direction, but which invariably over time leads the nation toward a higher state of material wealth and social well-being. At the heart of that change is the evolutionary notion of the form and functions of government and its role in American society. The interesting paradox is how American government has become at the same time more local and global.

> **Denver Chronicle April 14, 2013:**
>
> GPS and "Talking Shoes" Guide Toddler Home Safely

The post-World War II period through about 1980 was a time of large, centralized and activist government. In many respects, big government served our country well in this era. We rebuilt Europe and staved off Communism. Government spending and incentives helped transition U.S. society and a burgeoning civilian workforce from a war to a peace economy. The strong federal government desegregated the South and put a man on the moon. The limits of the government became clear with the stagflation of the 1970s and the increasing inability of the federal government to respond to challenges that demanded local solutions. I am talking about schools, land use, commerce, health care, the environment, and a federal debt burden that threatened to weigh heavily on the backs of future generations of Americans.

Increasingly, starting in the early 1980s, tax, spending and program management responsibilities devolved to states and local governments. Amazingly, this dynamic was not reversed, and by some measures it accelerated under Democratic leadership from the early 1990s through the early 2000s. Why? Because, in short, devolution worked for the majority of Americans. Its success is evident in more sensitive and responsive government, greater efficiencies and lower taxes. It is indeed hard to argue with success, especially when its foundations appear solid and its sustainability seems assured.

With devolution, the enterprise of government grew more manageable—and effective. As in industry, better products and services emerged as the government got closer to its stakeholder "customers." As with industry, huge efficiencies were realized as information technology was absorbed into all the processes of government. Government could do much more with much less and the robust economy allowed an unprecedented degree of bureaucratic shrinkage from Washington to county seats across the country. Everyone benefited.

2. Federal Power Redefined

Devolution has worked not because government has shirked from its responsibilities, but rather because it has conducted its affairs with greater intelligence, foresight and restraint. Which is *not* the same as the extreme libertarian view that government in general and especially Washington should get out of the way—in an absolute sense—of private forces in the marketplace. Had devolution evolved in this way, I am convinced we would have had greater social inequality, a crumbling and noncompetitive infrastructure and, without meaningful incentives, significantly less innovation and technological progress.

Here in the U.S., federal organizational support and financial incentives for high-risk ventures have been crucial. The fact that a lot of risk-sharing consortia have led, for example, the big ticket space projects, should not obscure the fact that without U.S. government involvement, there would have been no consortia formed to begin with. The commercial risks would have been unmanageable.

In the past, the U.S. taxpayers covered a large (and I believe) unreasonable piece of this risk. The difference today is that risk is much more widely, and wisely, shared. For example, the old NASA, as you know, no longer exists. Its reincarnation as a seemingly larger and more powerful organization known as NASCA (National Aeronautics, Space, and Communications Administration) represents, in fact, a radical shrinkage of operational responsibilities for this federal administration. This is especially true in the R&D area, where large, private and horizontally networked firms collaborate on large NASCA contracts. They share risks, they share rewards, under complex formulas which blend financial returns, intellectual property rights, and first-use guarantees. This difference has turned out to be an amazingly successful incentive system, with analogs today throughout the economy, and with quite a bit to show for them, including the discovery in 2004 of an AIDS vaccine.

Finally, we need to recognize the benefits of an activist foreign policy in the new century. Despite the near absence of traditional security threats, the U.S. has no less a stake in influencing (if not controlling) what happens outside our borders. In large part, we assert ourselves not unilaterally but multilaterally, through International Organizations and Private Non-Governmental Organizations. One of these IOs, the Global Economic Commission, must be recognized as having played a critical role in sustaining the liberal trading order that has brought us so much economic security and prosperity. U.S. support for the Commission has been essential to its success. This support is the kind of initiative that requires strong, visionary government leadership and that even the most powerful and enlightened corporate forces cannot provide. Trust me on this one.

As my fellow panelist, Dr. Mukerjee, will doubtless emphasize, America's good fortunes are not universally shared and, in fact, some of our blessings are now, for our neighbors, nothing less than curses. This compels us to be involved in the world and to influence these challenging transitions positively.

3. Prominent New Actors and Allies

My third observation is actually a set of observations about the new actors that have emerged on the scene, domestically and internationally.

Predictably, given my day job, I believe the single most important set of actors on the global stage, after governments, are global corporations. They are today the most powerful vehicles for trade, technology and knowledge transfer, direct investment, and human capital development in the global economy. In large measure, present and planned space expeditions are being directed by consortia of the world's leading technology firms. In the high-tech realm, few successful start-ups can resist the deep pockets of these large, global powerhouses and remain independent for long. Minimally, firms need to be affiliated and/or networked with the big global players.

In contrast to past images of multinational organizations, global companies today are truly global. They are horizontally integrated, with boards of directors representative of the countries in which firms conduct their business. Even IBM's board much more closely resembles "what the rest of the world looks like." Global companies make it their business to manage government relations expertly. When they do not, the consequence can be devastating, judging by the recent penalties against the four European space contractors convicted of bribery and unethical competitive activities. Going forward, it is important to recognize that the risk of unethical business practices of this nature is enormous given the size and clout of large organizations, the reduction in government oversight and watchdog activities, and the highly charged competitive environment in which companies do business.

The next category of key stakeholders is IOs and NGOs. The rise in influence of International Organizations (IOs) and affiliated Non-Governmental Organizations (NGOs), particularly in the areas of dispute resolution, advocacy, economic adjustment, development assistance, standards setting and technology transfer, is salient. Twenty years ago, these functions were considered by the U.S. and many of our allies as key tools of foreign policy for sovereign powers. Today, the leading states of the world have ceded considerable policy and operational authority to them, with few obviously detrimental effects. Nationalism, of course, still exists. It just no longer blinds most nations—and I would include the U.S.– to the benefits of multilateralism and regionalism. Not surprisingly perhaps, substantive progress on a vast array of delicate international issues has advanced in direct proportion to the authority ceded to the IOs. Consider the success of multilateralism in global law enforcement, including drug interdiction, money laundering, and human rights monitoring.

My final observation centers on Political Affinity Groups and the ascendance of digital democracy. Two decades ago, the thought of virtual voting conjured up fearful images of Orwellian manipulation at the hands of diabolical demagogues. While overblown, the risk of manipulation existed. As always, what was not anticipated were the market and societal responses to the new technology. For example, in time for the 2008 presidential election, PAGs—or Political Affinity Groups—came on the scene to help fill the need for order and coherence, and to provide competing sources of issue information. Many of you, I assume, are affiliated with one or more PAGs. (I am.) The PAGs help explain public policy issues and in effect mediate electronic voter responses across a wide range of issues. Voters are still not as well read on specific issues; but they are not easily duped, either. Most will agree the electorate is better informed, and more engaged in the political process as a result.

Question: You haven't said anything about the energy revolution brought about by Solantai. Isn't this breakthrough the key to our wealth and progress?

Answer: No, as much as it has contributed greatly to economic welfare practically all over the world, I argue that Solantai is the result and not the cause of our progress for this reason: The secret of Solantai would not have been unlocked without a major, global development effort that involved significant cooperation, technology exchanges and risk sharing among the participating firms from the U.S. and Japan. Without this effort, there would be no Solantai, no cheap energy, more pollution, more resource problems. Thank you. I'll leave it at that, as I have a hunch the next speaker, Dr. Cullinane, will have a thing or two to say about Solantai as well!

Solantai: A Perspective on The Great Energy Breakthrough

By Dr. Padraic Cullinane

Dr. Cullinane is Professor of Electrical Engineering at Trinity College, Dublin and head of the Energy Technology Task Force of the Global Economic Commission. He is also a technical advisor to UNSTAD and the European Union's Energy Development and Transfer program. His presentation was delivered via satellite.

Good day. I regret that I must be a virtual contributor and cannot be with you in the real, carbon sense. A decade or more ago, as a young professional, I was often forced to resort to satellite participation (which by the way was primitive by comparison with today) because of a chronic tendency to be overbooked and overcommitted. I am happy to say that this schedule conflict is a rather happy one, as I am in the midst of a six month leave during which time I will be relaxing, spending time at home with my family, catching up on some professional reading and, of all things, studying painting in France! I mention all this to make the point that my virtual participation in this symposium, while on leave and having time to personally and intellectually "refresh",

> **The New York Times, July 17, 2018:**
>
> **University Space Station Anounces Commencement Ceremony Date for First Graduating Class**

is itself an important image of the present age, is it not?

As you know, I am here to discuss the broad social and economic implications of the extraordinary breakthrough of R-170 or, as it is popularly known, Solantai.

First, some background.

As most in this audience are well aware, Solantai is essentially a process for capturing and transmitting solar energy from space to earth. A Czech-American, Dr. Peter Glaser, achieved the first major theoretical breakthrough in 1968. Further research was conducted by the U.S. Department of Energy and (what was then) NASA in the late 1970s. Using the technology of that time, the DOE-NASA study created a "1979 Reference System" design for solar power satellites. This system comprised a group of 60 large platforms in geo-stationary Earth orbit, each to deliver 5 gigawatts of power via wireless power transmission using a microwave beam. The image was unbelievably ambitious, especially for that time. Each platform would power one large U.S. city, linking to the existing power grid! The system would have cost $265 billion (1999 dollars) and would have taken 20 years to develop and implement. Not surprisingly, work on the project stopped in the early 1980s because of the high cost, waning public interest as the energy crisis passed, and large technological risk.

In 1995-1997, NASA (now, NASCA, the National Aeronautics, Space and Communication Administration) conducted a "Fresh Look" study. This study proposed a "brilliant" system, capable of self-assembly in space using mass-produced parts. The study concluded that solar power from space seriously should be reconsidered.

In the first decade of the 21st century, NASCA's strategic goal of greatly reduced cost of access to space was attained, thanks largely to increased involvement of the private sector in the space program. This goal led to a joint U.S./Japan energy project that produced the huge breakthrough which you all know about in 2006. The breakthrough was the feasibility of beaming solar energy via satellites to earth. NASCA then shifted its priority from a manned mission to Mars to Solantai and began to implement the system. The implementation was performed by horizontally-integrated companies competing against one another to best implement system components according to NASCA specifications. Electric utilities themselves designed and built the receiving sites that converted the beamed microwave energy into standard electrical power and supplied it to the power grid. The rest is history.

Technological Implications

Similar to the Apollo program of the 1960s, the development of Solantai has led to many technological advances. Low-noise electronic microwave devices, power electronics, high-efficiency, low-mass photovoltaic cells, and aerospace technology advanced as large investments were made to implement the system. New lift vehicles have been developed to carry the payloads into orbit, and with this technology the cost and risk of launching all types of satellites have decreased. As a result, satellite bandwidth has become incredibly cheap and like the cost of energy, the cost of global communications has fallen to practically zero.

In addition, advances have been made in "brilliant" systems that can assemble themselves automatically. This technology will facilitate the habitation of space by reducing the amount of equipment and labor needed to construct systems in space. This same technology is being applied on earth as products are designed to manufacture themselves.

Environmental Implications

The environmental implications of Solantai have been profound. Fossil fuels have not been replaced entirely, but otherwise excessive reliance on them has been reduced. This reduction has resulted in lower CO_2 emissions and a diminished greenhouse effect. New effects such as the heating of the atmosphere by the beamed energy has caused minor climate changes, but this effect has been lower than that caused by 20th century CO_2 emissions.

Alternative sources of energy such as land-based solar panels and geothermal energy do not increase the heat flow from outer space into the earth's atmosphere. Solantai, however, causes the earth to receive more energy from space than it presently does, resulting in slightly higher temperatures. Notwithstanding the surprising and at times violent resistance Solantai has sparked from what I call the paranoid Green fringe, it is very much a net positive sum game for Mother Earth.

There are some aesthetic issues, as you know. To be exposed to sunlight continuously, and to permit fixed receiving sites without the complexity of tracking mechanisms, the 60 satellites (assuming 5,000 MW each) are in GEO (geostationary earth orbit) on the equatorial plane. These satellites have associated with them other environmental effects that were not experienced with traditional energy systems. For example, Solantai satellites are large and are observable by the naked eye in the nighttime sky. (I am aware that some people object to this visual pollution.) Another issue is that orbital space has become scarce because of minimum spacing requirements between satellites to prevent interference with communications satellites. This last problem will eventually require international cooperation to allocate limited orbital space.

Economic Implications

Who are the economic beneficiaries of Solantai?
Directly or indirectly, we are all beneficiaries.

With relatively few exceptions, econometric models show conclusively that living standards around the world have increased as consumers spend less money on more energy. It is cheaper to make things, and it is cheaper to move things. Air transport costs plummeted as jet fuel could be synthesized cheaply from the basic elements of carbon and hydrogen using Solantai-transmitted energy. Electric cars, which had been introduced unsuccessfully at the turn of the millennium, have become technologically and commercially viable since Solantai has catalyzed long-awaited breakthroughs in battery technology (which will eventually allow full-size electric cars to travel 500 miles on a single 5 minute charge costing under $10). Consumers are happier and their air is cleaner thanks to Solantai. This is particularly true in the high energy-consuming developed nations, like Japan, which are otherwise extremely dependent on expensive imported energy.

Solantai has advanced the economic cause of emerging nations as well, however. The growth rate of the GDP of developing countries has accelerated as these countries have been transformed into manufacturing and/or satellite launch centers, or have simply received more generous aid from prosperous donor countries. The key point is that developing countries face challenges in gaining access to the system, but enjoy huge benefits once they can tap into Solantai.

Balancing this is the reality that Solantai has undermined the traditional energy markets. The availability of very cheap energy has reduced the demand for oil and natural gas, depressing their price, and creating a lot of political challenges in the countries most directly affected, including Saudi Arabia, Iran, Kazakhstan, Azerbaijan, and, closer to home, Venezuela and Mexico.

Infrastructure Implications

Solantai has surfaced a range of land and land-use issues. Consider this: A typical 5,000 MW receiving site requires approximately 150 km^2 of land area depending on distance from the equator, including a two kilometer buffer zone around the perimeter of the site. Regions of high population density have opted to implement the receiving sites offshore due to land area constraints. While expected breakthroughs in room temperature superconductors will allow smaller receiving sites, today, in the year 2020, the state of the technology only allows such superconductors to be used in low power applications.

Most developing countries are located in equatorial regions. To have fixed receiving sites, the satellites must be geostationary and thus located above the equator. The good news here is that developing countries are able to use much smaller and cheaper receiving sites and therefore enjoy a lower cost of power than those countries located further north or south. We have seen in the past decade how the change in the power equation has greatly accelerated industrial development in Southeast Asia, China and Brazil. Cheaper power is clearly an incentive for more industrial development. This fact is creating a sustainable competitive advantage in energy-intensive industries, like steel and automotives, for companies operating in equatorial countries.

Now, I do not mean to suggest that Solantai alone has the power to uplift the poorest of poor countries and succeed where billions of dollars of aid and assistance have failed. Solantai is no panacea for such countries. While the marginal costs of energy from Solantai is low, there is a large fixed cost associated with implementing the system. Large payments to foreign companies constructing the system would drain scarce foreign exchange reserves in some countries. Those countries that are not able to pay the large up-front cost (about $5 billion) continue to rely on traditional energy sources, foreign investment, or aid from richer countries. They hope to some day have the means to tap into the power of Solantai.

In conclusion, Solantai is by far the most important discovery since the personal computer. I am convinced its future role will only grow more important, particularly as we venture deeper into space exploration, manufacturing and eventual colonization. Thank you.

Question: Does Solantai create new security risks?

I am frequently asked if Solantai has rendered us more vulnerable to terrorism. Like most other power generation systems, Solantai is vulnerable to military attack, either by attacking the receiving sites, attacking the satellites themselves, or by disrupting the beam between the satellites and the receiving sites. The receiving sites do not make good military targets, however, because they are large and are composed of redundant elements. As such, they probably are less prone to attack than are fossil fuel power plants. The launch vehicles themselves may be an easier target because they are susceptible to heat seeking missiles.

On the other side, Solantai has limited military uses; specifically, to jam radio communications by redirecting and concentrating the microwave beam, and by providing large-scale power to remote military sites. It is important to bear in mind that any use as a weapon would violate space treaties and make the system itself a military target, so such use has not been pursued.

Furthermore, in this time of prosperity and peace, security issues do not command as high a priority as they otherwise might.

Prospects for Global Prosperity
By Amir Mukerjee

Dr. Mukerjee is a fellow on leave from the MIT's Economics Department while serving a two-year term as Visiting Scholar at the Global Economic Commission.

I have greatly enjoyed the two preceding presentations. They leave me feeling optimistic and hopeful, which is consistent with my world and life outlook. I have several comments, which have mostly to do with the global implications of what my good friend Dr. Davis calls "The Unexpected American Renaissance."

First, America has truly been the model for 21st century political and economic organization throughout much of the world, including Asia and the developing world. It did not look like this would be the case in the early years of the new century. Growth was sluggish, the stock market underwent a larger than anticipated "correction" in 2003, and many predicted an extended period of malaise and uncertainty. But the correction turned out to be relatively short-lived downward blip because in my opinion the U.S. had the fiscal and monetary fundamentals right, together with the fact that we (and I now mean the world) were on the verge of several technological breakthroughs, by far the most important of which has been, as you know, Solantai.

Much of the rest of the world is now catching up. Arguably the five largest EU members combined have already done so. Solantai has significantly leveled the playing field and removed barriers to entry into the international division of labor. How will this shake out over the next ten years? With vibrant economic growth and rising affluence, the U.S. may not mind being merely first among economic equals. What if growth slows? Will the U.S. maintain its openness?

Second, Solantai's potential contribution to global growth and development is extraordinarily exciting. Yet in the absence of massive aid and "change leadership" (political development, institutional reform, and so on.), all the energy in the universe will do little to alter the fundamental economic challenges of places like Africa and Central America. We saw this happen in Africa with the eradication of AIDS. This event was a great feat, but in many nations hardships and political instability continued post-AIDS eradication and continue to be with us today.

Third, we must bear in mind that some areas are suffering rather acutely from the so-called New Economy brought about by Solantai. We are witnessing today the continued fallout in the Middle East from the collapse of traditional energy markets. Saudi

Arabia and Iran clearly did not have the diversified economies or the means to transition to themselves, even with external aid, to new forms of production and participation in the world economy. So, it is hardly surprising that that region of the world is the center of such political instability and uncertainty, and that it continues to export practitioners of, shall I say, extremist politics, to the rest of the world.

Even more troubling is Russia's inability to politically and economically adjust. Our collective naiveté was profound, believing as we did back in the early 1990s that several billion dollars in aid and the formal adoption of democratic processes would undo decades of communist policies. Russia failed to get its economic house in order and then, as we know one of its few real assets—Caspian Sea oil—was permanently devalued by Solantai. The impact has been understandably devastating. If the West has solved its own domestic welfare problems, it has enabled a new welfare client in Russia! The fact that the U.S., EU and China convinced Russia a decade ago to decommission its nuclear arsenal in exchange for a prominent role in the space effort does not leave me reassured. There are still too many discontented and frustrated people with too much time on their hands there. Many of the most talented of these are card-carrying members of global crime syndicates.

My final point relates to my own personal concerns over the integrity and security of information and content in an era of almost universal connectivity, and with so few access restrictions. Intellectual property is, as you know, the essence of value in today's economy and the Global Net is the depository and transmission vehicle for ideas, formulas, plans and blueprints. Are we correct in believing that existing protections and safeguards are effective, and that they will be in the future? There are clever people out there who are ruthless in their determination to get the upper hand in this highly competitive global economy of ours. If you don't believe me, ask the people involved in the IBM-Hitachi consortium, which may have lost $2 billion in business recently when its proposal for the V-77 space launch support system appeared inexplicably on public space on the Global Net for all to see. It is not the traditional mischief-making hackers I fear, but rather increasingly powerful organized crime elements whose technical capabilities give them the ability to steal and resell information and trade secrets to the ultimate detriment of our workers and their employers.

I fear that a lot more of this kind of info crime is taking place than is officially acknowledged. I suspect that corporations are too concerned about the downside effects on their reputation if they report it. A broad-based loss of Net confidence could be highly detrimental to the global economy and, even worse, it could undermine the trust and confidence between nations and major stakeholders that have evolved over the last two decades.

I hope in my comments and questions that I have not rained on your parade. Let me reaffirm my credentials as an optimist by saying in conclusion that the world economy has never before enjoyed such great prospects for sustainable and equitable growth. But there is work to be done and we will only arrive at each higher stage of development when we have recognized and come to grips with the challenges that our wonderful and hopeful future presents us.

Thank you.

YANKEE GOING HOME

SUMMARY

Who runs things? Why are decisions made and what goalsare being pursued? Who are our friends and our enemies? Just what is going on in the world? In 2020 you could be forgiven asking those questions because little is clear except that the world has changed in fundamental ways. The U.S. has withdrawn from the world, gone home, after a series of terrible foreign policy blunders and a long-standing and deep recession. The world is heavily influenced by the memories of terrorism, war, and instability that followed U.S. isolationism. In the wake of the U.S. retreat we find a world made up of both traditional actors (nations, international organizations) and powerful non-traditional actors (global corporate alliances, criminal groups, mercenary units). They cooperate for power and influence and compete for position and control in a shifting calliope of politics and economics that is bewildering to nearly all. In this world traditional notions of allegiance are questioned and the "rules of the game" are difficult to understand.

The Toronto Studios of World Syncom, 12 March 2020

These holo studio chairs may be designed to keep your posture looking great from all angles, but they're damn uncomfortable.

Amanda cringed inwardly. The techs were preparing to turn on those awesome lights. I hate those lights. Ah, but three more interviews and then a vacation at the new Starwoods-Virgin resort in Kenya, she thought.

Great news from her publishers, yesterday. I can afford that resort! Her netpub firm, Vance & Odell, had just confirmed her account status. Every time someone downloaded her book, five Euros were added to her growing wealth. Let's see—about 550,000 downloads at the last accounting. She liked that number; she liked the economics of netpubs. And even more startling, her paperpub was going into a third printing. She knew she had a knack for writing that made academic subjects interesting. She was also savvy enough to appreciate that her good looks played well on netcasts, since no one expected a Ph.D. in Global Politics to look anything but stodgy. That probably helped sales, too.

On the down side, she thought, my personal revenue taxes have taken a huge jump in the wrong direction. And it is so weird to pay my taxes to a private firm. It always seemed natural when non-essential government functions, like air traffic control or education, were privatized, but now that revenue collection is run by private firms…! Well, in some ways I guess I like it. If I pay my obligations off in advance, I get a discount. And Goldman Sachs Visa does a great job of rolling up all my global tax obligations into one account. I wish the US would join in. They have privatized a lot of functions, like their FAA, NASA, and Health and Welfare, but not tax collection.

But for all that enhanced income, Dr. Amanda Krause had begun to wonder just what was going on. Why this enormous popularity?

Vance & Odell were well known for their political ties with some powerful Globals, especially those that want to curtail the use of mercenary forces. This popularity of mine could be an illusion; a contrived affair to manipulate some political scheme about which I am totally ignorant. Five years ago, that thought would have seemed far-fetched, but no longer. Her research into the fall of the U.S., the Byzantine, almost incomprehensible, global political system that followed, and the rise of the era of the Global Corporations had given her a very healthy respect for the political skills of the Globals.

Here comes the Director with the same old speech. I could give it myself after a three-month publicity tour. "Please speak distinctly for the autotranslator.

"Normal jargon is okay. Be sure to look around like you are in a living room. Never forget that they can see you from all sides and angles. Don't worry about modesty. Our algorithms digitally reformat the front and top views when necessary. Always try to favor looking at the old flat screen cameras at stage front. Much of the global market, and especially the U.S., still uses flat screen technology." The director gave the speech almost has she had predicted, than added that holoing would begin in twenty minutes.

That was fine with her. The "director's speech," as she thought of it, had set her on a new train of thought. Autotranslators and digital reformatting – I wonder just how much of what I say is really heard or seen around the world? How much is altered to suit some Globals' agenda? Let's see. World Syncom owns this facility and they are aligned politically and in business with Networld, the key distributor here in North America. Both companies, in alliance with GM and Deutsche Bank, recently signed monetary stabilization and trade augmentation agreements with the U.S., Canada, and Brazil. My analysis would help make their case with other countries that are considering similar agreements.

I wonder if the popularity of my book has something to do with nostalgia? It has been nearly fifteen years since the U.S. shrank from its world role. A generation of school children has grown up without a U.S. superpower. My book does draw some pretty stark distinctions between the American Era and the present. Not that life was all that great with the Americans dominating things! But at least you knew how things worked! It was clear who made decisions. It was clear why decisions were made. In the 1990s at least you knew who the key global actors were and how and why they exercised power.

Are people getting wistful for the predictability of the old days? Or do they just want today's system explained a bit better? Hmm, my book actually fills both of those roles. Now, whose political power agenda is advanced by that public attitude? They would do what they could to bolster sales – the show sponsors, certainly. I should have thought through the implications of this before. This whirlwind celebrity life I've been leading has put my analytical side to sleep.

Well, another time. Here comes my interviewer. He is much older and shorter in person. That's what digital reformatting can do for you, I guess. Alex Meade is a famous netcaster within the Ford-Motorola-Chelomei-Ling Alliance. It's interesting that they loaned him out for a public netcast. Okay, its time to earn another 25,000 downloads.

Alex Meade introduced himself (although they had met a week earlier) and apologized for not being at the pre-show an hour before. That was unusual and perhaps it explained why he seemed nervous.

"Lights in one minute," said the Director. Amanda cringed.
"I thought we could run through some history, first," said Meade.

"American isolationism means that they believe a distorted version of why they are a second-rate power."

"Scrubbers coming on," said a voice off stage (dust particles are the bane of holocasting).

"That may be a bit of an overstatement, Alex. The U.S. is still a crucial player and a very important market. Why else would the GM-Deutsche Bank Group be so intent on treaties with the U.S. to help maintain global market stability?" Amanda replied.

The Directors voice came up again, "Sound check complete. Lasing on. Pickups on. Flat screen cameras running. We are live in fifteen seconds."

"Good evening, everyone. I'm Alex Meade and I have the pleasure of spending the next hour with the famous author Dr. Amanda Krause. For those of you who don't know her, Dr. Krause is the author of one of the most-widely read netpubs of the past decade, *Some Might Call It Business.* This netcast is brought to you free of any charges, including high bandwidth surcharges, by the Sony-Anaconda Corporate Alliance, United States Public Netcasting, the North Atlantic Corporate Coalition, the Government of Brazil, and the Wall Street-Fleet Street Confederation. Secure logistics and personal protective services have been donated by WorldWide Spetz. Just a reminder—you don't have to view any commercials to reduce or eliminate your access charges, but product and service advertising is available at the touch of the Euro icon on your screen."

"Dr. Krause – Amanda – your book has been enormously popular, yet it poses some controversial notions. For example, you assert that we owe our globally affluent lives today to the perseverance of the United States twenty years ago. However, most would say that U.S. actions in the early 2000s took the world to the brink of chaos; that we owe our affluence to the power and wisdom of the Globals."

What a brown nose, she thought. She had been watching Alex. He was glued to the holo-prompters that floated behind her head. She could see them by reflection. There are far more prompters than usual and they seem to have contingency questions and answers on them. Oh! He hasn't read my book! Someone is feeding him stuff. There is an edge I can use.

"Tell me, Alex," she answered. "What was your least favorite part of my book?" His prompters were mostly blank. He looked panicked. "That's okay, Alex, I'm sure you liked it all." No one anticipated that question. Now he knows that I know.

"Actually, Alex, the only reason people might disagree with me is because they are not making some important temporal distinctions. For almost fifty years, the U.S. Government was a lone voice in the world trying to educate everyone on the virtues of a global outlook – free trade, freedom of movement, and open markets. That the U.S. economy would benefit from such a world was neither here nor there. The fact is the U.S. slowly pushed, prodded, cajoled, and led the world kicking and screaming into the kind of porous borders and global market culture we take for granted in 2020."

"So why did the U.S. misstep? What happened?"

"Alex, don't think of it has a misstep. That gives the wrong impression. The U.S. made mistakes, certainly. Largely they were the mistakes that come from arrogance. But the key to change, especially the massive paradigm-shifting change we have experienced since about 2012, does not come from a mistake. It comes from large, almost irresistible, global forces for change– social, political, economic, and ideological. Indeed, in many ways the U.S. was a victim of its huge successes."

"Amanda, you realize that what you say seems preposterous to most of the world. The average global citizen sees the U.S. as foolish, bumbling, and impotent with a Government that can barely see past its own borders. The more affluent and well-educated Americans are torn. They have competing allegiances between the country where they happened to be born and the Globals who offer them security, intellectual challenges and a sense of value for what they can contribute. The American working class lives with the threat of unemployment, personal insecurity, and the loss of the 'American Dream' every day. They are fixated on netcasts that glorify the past. They are nationalistic and insecure. How can that be a function of their own success?" Interesting how he switches back and forth between an American accent when he asks questions and a Globals accent when he dumps on the U.S.

Meade is good; slimy, but good. "Okay, let me just tick off for you some key observations about the early 2000s."

Amanda touched a micro switch on her watchband to activate the UltraPoint graphic that viewers could see. The WatchAssist was a gift from the Sony Corporation (one of the show sponsors). With the foldout screen in her briefcase, it was a multi-function computing assistant and communicator. Through speech input, she could even operate her home computer for remote typing, data management, and mail. Now she was using it to control the studio projection equipment. A holo image shimmered between them.

"The U.S. was doing far more than many realized. The restructuring of the Japanese economy was making real progress thanks to U.S. help. The South Asian economies, hit so hard in the late 1990s, had made significant strides as a result of U.S. consulting support and American corporate investment.

The Euro was not doing well, but the U.S. was adjusting its policies to prop it up. There was relative peace in the Middle East. Latin American legal and structural reforms were bringing some solid growth to the region, again with U.S. support. In other words, the U.S. was doing all the things necessary to boost global growth outside the U.S. and encourage the globalization of corporations."

"However, people over the world began to feel resentment at the longstanding U.S. pre-eminence. Westernization brought the good and the ills of market economies. Crime, drugs, materialism, higher levels of personal uncertainty, and the erosion of traditional values

---

The Year 2005 Global Power Structure

- *Nation-States are the only legitimate users of political power*

- *The U.S. is guaranteeing global stability and diplomatic, economic, and military power*

- *Several Regional Wars have been won with amazingly low costs in U.S. lives*

- *The U.S. is successfully pushing a global agenda:*

  √ *Free Trade*
  √ *Enviromentalism*
  √ *Global capital markets*
  √ *Regional stability treaties*
  √ *Encouraging U.S. Corporations to invest abroad*

- *The Global Internet and e-business are driven by American initiatives*

---

and power structures accompanied increased wealth, education and opportunity. The U.S. global position was actually weaker than it appeared on the surface."

"But surely, Amanda, the real cause of the chaos and terrorism of the 2010s was the ineptitude of the U.S. military."

"Mr. Meade, I realize it is your job to be provocative, but that is a very sophomoric analysis (you jerk) and I am surprised that you would subscribe to it. Sure, the U.S. military had become a bit complacent. But it was the policy makers in Washington that set up the U.S. for failure – first, by delaying weapon system upgrades and, second, by losing the propaganda war. The Philippine Insurrection began in 2004 with a "self-determination" revolution in the north. Remember, the U.S. committed a huge force to the Philippines over the next year and eventually won by 2006,

---

Problems Arising for the 00's Global Power Source

- *Global capital flows and currency values were getting out of Government control*

- *Emerging market countries very successfully lured U.S. and European Corporations out of their home countries*

- *The U.S. Military became over-enamored of hi-tech and lost force projection capabilities at the same time that many of its platforms had become outdated*

- *The global arms market expanded with the increased power of global crime organizations*

- *Significant backlashes against Western consumerism started in several regions*

- *The U.S. was arrogant about its position, believing nothing could significantly harm U.S. interests*

---

although this time with numerous casualties. They got the political solution they wanted between the Government and the Moslem insurgents. So, where was the failure? It was in the propaganda war. The Moslems of the world were outraged at the U.S. actions. They portrayed the U.S. as a bumbling and mean-spirited bully, as an imperial power that was suppressing Islamic freedom. The imagery stuck".

"Losing that image battle on the world political stage was bad enough, but as we know the next incident went a long way to prove (seemingly) the assertions being made about the U.S. Taking advantage of U.S. engagement in the Pacific, the Iraqi Government swept into Kuwait. This time they portrayed themselves as ridding the Gulf region of a U.S. puppet. Local powers acquiesced. The U.S. could get no allied support for a Kuwaiti rescue and, being engaged in the Pacific, had few forces to spare of its own. A small task force was sent to cruise the area to back up diplomatic efforts and stand by to take out Americans. Was it inadequate training? An inexperienced Captain? Faulty sensors? We will never know, since both ships were destroyed. It does appear the American destroyer fired first, probably at what they thought was an attacking Iraqi submarine. It was an Iranian submarine and before being hit, it got off a return shot that sunk the Americans."

"The Iranians closed the Straits of Hormuz to all U.S. destination vessels and the Saudis went along with it. Illegal? Yes. Justifiable in the eyes of the world? Yes. Another example of the bumbling imperialistic Americans attacking Islam? You bet. Humiliating to every American citizen? Everyone compared it to the failed Iranian hostage rescue of the 1970s. From the U.S. view, the world spiraled down out of control from that point on."

At this point, Meade broke in. "At this dramatic recounting, we will take a short break. We will be back with Amanda Krause in ten minutes. The icons on your screens will lead you to historical information sources and combat footage as well as upcoming netcasts, commercials, and product surveys and lotteries by our sponsors.

The Troubles: 2004 - 2008

- *The Philippine Insurrection with outside support, and U.S. intervention*

- *The U.S. loses the propaganda war*

- *The rise of U.S. terrorism, especially against U.S. corporations abroad*

- *The Iranian naval incident*

- *The U.S. recession*

- *The Saudi Arabian coup*

He got instructions to break early. I wonder if some Global exec was afraid that my story was a bit too sympathetic to the U.S. They don't want the U.S. to be seen in too favorable a light. It might call too many things into question. Meade seems anxious to speak with me. "Excuse me, won't you Mr. Meade? I need to stretch my legs." Well, here comes my "driver." Boy that woman never gets far away. She really takes this protective service seriously. Who does she think she's protecting me from, a jealous irate historian?

"Excuse me, Doctor," said Lieutenant Morran. "If you're taking a walk, may I join you?"

"Of course," replied Amanda, " I'm delighted to have the company (and it will keep that idiot Meade at a distance), but it's only a ten minute break."

"Thank you Dr. Krause, and before I forget, I will join you immediately after the show. That will keep that Meade character at arm's length." Jeez, am I that easy to read? Lt. Morran guided

Amanda over near some electrical equipment and without a word removed Amanda's WatchAssist, placed it on the floor and they walked away. "You never know," she said. By which, I take it that the Lieutenant knows very well that Sony has me bugged. Damn.

"Doctor, my Colonel would like an appointment to speak with you about becoming a political consultant to the regiment. I can see that surprises you. My only orders are to try to make an appointment, Dr. Krause, but let me say something off the record. Colonel Schroeder is well aware that you dislike mercenaries. Quite frankly, he thinks you're a bit naive. However, you will find him in total agreement with you about the dangers posed by global mercenary units. Doctor, within some very high corporate circles and within certain relatively ambitious mercenary units, there are studies underway right now examining the feasibility in the future for mercenary armies to contest economic and political issues on the battlefield with national armed forces. You don't look totally surprised. Maybe you are the right person for this job. Colonel Schroeder is worried about this trend. He does not like it or agree with it. He wants some help in understanding it. Can I report that you will favor him with an interview?"

Amanda found herself nodding her head yes, without much thought. Well talking can't hurt. Can it? What a night! Colonel Schroeder actually has a pretty good reputation and Worldwide Spetz is known to be a class act; odd considering its origins. "You're not really a protective service driver or a lieutenant are you? Have you been in Spetz intelligence very long?" Okay, pretend you don't hear me.

A production assistant rushed up. "Here is your WatchAssist Doctor Krause. It must have fallen off. Let me put it on for you. These things are amazing. I wish I could afford one. Then I would never be out of touch." You don't know the half of it, she thought.

Amanda sat back down and let her mind wonder. Boy, I really do need that vacation! Now I'm doubly glad that George can join me. I can talk to my little brother about anything. She started thinking about the life that George had chosen. He originally joined the Bechtel-Kawanzia Group as a hard charging GMBA-Civil Engineer. His first assignment had been postponed and B-K asked him to do some teaching in the interim. He ended up in their Educational Foundation with a teaching assignment in Zambia. He hasn't been the same since. The guy has an amazing gift for helping people, and B-K let him run with it. I'm so proud of him. He even decided to leave B-K for full-time charity work. Instead B-K kept him on "staff" and seeded his new African Development Foundation with its first five hundred million Euros. Since that day, he has found the generosity of the Globals overwhelming. Sure they see future consumers in the success of his efforts, but that is a generation off. Right now, he is glad to be bringing a quality living standard to those in need. It is not unlike the generosity of the Globals toward the U.S. public education system. In many communities they pay teachers' salaries, buy computers and books, provide free breakfast programs, and repair buildings. It may be in their long-term interest, but they really are making a huge difference in people's lives. There was a time when people thought that only governments would take on public welfare issues.

Ah, the opposite of my brother. Here comes Meade back to the stage. He's looking a bit uneasy. "Everyone set," said the director. Meade was poised to ask his next question.

"So," said Amanda jumping right in, "lets recap where we left off." He looks nonplussed. Good. "As we moved into 2007, the U.S. was in a downward spiral. The country looked foolish and ineffectual to the world. Terrorist attacks on U.S. corporations and assets abroad had not stopped. There had been several terrorist incidents in the U.S. with significant loss of life. It was not surprising, of course, that all this instability hit the stock markets hard. Investors were losing confidence. By February of 2007, the Dow was down to 16,000, having lost 15 per cent of its value. Capital was fleeing abroad, mostly to Asia and Latin America. A recession hit hard and by June unemployment was up to 12 per cent. The mood of the American voter became increasing insecure and angry. They and their political leaders began to blame unnamed global forces. By the end of the year, it was clear that no one would win the next presidential election unless they sponsored isolationist policies."

"Very interesting , Amanda. So let's move on to…"

"The American voters got their wish. A very isolationist President and Congress were installed. Tariff and non-tariff barriers of various sorts were legislated. Embassy staffs were cut. Within six months, the WTO had made several rulings against the U.S. That further inflamed Americans. U.S. Armed Forces and their pre-positioned equipment were brought home. The defense budget was cut 20 per cent in the next couple of years. Across the world, the policeman everyone had taken for granted went home."

"Instability began to mount in various regions. The Philippine Insurrection rekindled. The Saudi Royal Family was overthrown. Kazakhstan declared itself an Islamic Republic and rejected all forms of alliance with Russia. Criminal organizations from Latin America to Russia to Asia began to operate openly and often violently. It was beginning to be hard to distinguish between rebels and criminals. Meanwhile, the U.S. recession deepened and American voters became more isolationist, especially as terrorist attacks on U.S. soil increased.

"It was during this time, around 2010, that the first glimmers of today's system began to emerge. Of course, no one appreciated it for what it was. It seemed just a small and justifiable step. Corporations around the globe were having serious security problems. Among terrorists, well-armed and well-funded criminal organizations, weak law enforcement, and increasing industrial espionage, they were being threatened, extorted and attacked. They began to beef up their corporate security forces or request that their security services upgrade their capabilities. Many ex-U.S. Special Forces members found new employment. To do their jobs better, the security services began sharing information with each other. Within a year, many of the world's largest corporations were sharing data and plans with partners, business rivals, and companies in unrelated markets. They began talking seriously about politics and social stability, not just business. Remember these discussions and early plans were not just targeted at 'outside forces.' Corporations had begun to prey on each other with industrial espionage, and various forms of cyber crime—theft of technology secrets, false e-mails, access to marketing data, etc. The great secure intranets of our time also began then."

"So," said Meade, trying to regain some control of his show, "that was the origins of today's system of multi-lateral corporate alliances, mercenary services, and waning governments?"

"No, Mr. Meade, numerous other events had to play out. Today's system was not inevitable at that time. I would say that three things changed our world forever."

"And for the better, I'm sure," said Meade.

Unbelievable brown nose. Ignoring him, Amanda continued, "The first is that the U.S. stayed permanently disengaged. That was crucial. Despite its problems, only the U.S. had the wherewithal to assert global leadership and re-establish stability on traditional lines. But the U.S. recession had gone on and on and the American public was insecure and lethargic. The U.S. budget had gone into serious deficit spending under a wide range of pressures for social safety net spending and job creation. The military budget, already about 60% of its 2005 figure, no longer kept pace with inflation each year as Congress tended to micro manage anything with a foreign flavor.

"The second factor was that no serious regional actors emerged to dominate parts of the globe. This was unprecedented in history. Normally when a hegemonic power retreats, local powers assert themselves. It did not happen. Why? I can name a number of reasons. She touched her WatchAssist again (noticing a certain reluctance on her part to use the infernal thing).

"Remember what this time was like. The U.N. was moving to Geneva. The OAS was moving to Brazil. NATO was in disarray. The World Bank was floundering. Most regional political alliances were discovering just how much they relied on the U.S. for leadership. None of the traditional avenues of international decisionmaking were operating. It also became evident that everyone had relied too much on U.S. agenda setting. People had lost the habits and skills of diplomatic leadership. No one stood up to replace the U.S. At the same time, global criminal elements used all the tools of their craft (bribery, extortion, murder, and theft) to derail any potentially successful movements to regional authority that might bring enhanced law enforcement. Finally, all national leaderships were very tightly focused on economic stimulation. Everyone was trying to pull the world out of recession without the engine of the U.S. market."

"The third factor that created our current system was not a large social force (like the others) but an event. The famous Singapore Letter of Marque. It started innocently enough. Several industrial leaders were having dinner with the Prime Minister of Singapore. The dinner discussion turned to piracy in the sea lanes of South East Asia. Everyone at the table suffered in one way or another from the extraordinary increase in regional piracy–trade was falling off, crews were hard to hire, insurance rates were skyrocketing, and cargo and ship losses were unsustainable. One of the executives at the table was an amateur historian, Sir Francis Hyde-Probert. In jest, he speculated that it was too bad that nations could no longer issue Letters of Marque, since his firm would gladly help finance a private warship to protect regional commerce. According to others at the dinner, everyone fell silent. The Prime Minister had an aide begin a research project immediately. Within three months the Malacca Alliance had been formed. It still exists today. Originally, they financed three fast patrol boats (leased from builders and local navies) with hired crews, mostly former U.S. Navy personnel (including a former SEAL team). Within two months, they captured a dozen pirate vessels and Singapore hanged the crews. Piracy dropped off remarkably. Within two years the Malacca Alliance, still under Letters of Marque (now from several countries), owned several ex-U.S. Navy frigates and helicopters and were a permanent

---

The Absence of Traditional Regional Powers 2008 - 2015

- *Traditional political infrastructures in transition or missing*

- *The habits of international statesmanship atrophied*

- *Crime and corruption worked to maintain the disorder that favored their activities*

- *Political attention was focused on pulling the world out of recession without the help of the U.S.*

---

sea lane patrol. They were financed by yearly subscriptions from local governments, insurers, and shipping firms. They made a profit after the third year of operation."

"Those three factors really started our current system off. Before long, corporations all over the world were forming alliances for mutual support, protection and market stability. In some places they actually began to perform some of the functions of Government. In most cases, however, they worked with local governments in a symbiotic relationship. Even the U.S. has not escaped the power of the Globals. In fact the U.S. remains tied to the world economy precisely because the Globals are multi-national market actors who tie everyone's economic activity together."

"What about Cuba, Dr. Krause?"

"Good point, Mr. Meade. Today we have eight kinds of international players. The one we haven't discussed is the Hybrid State. In 2016 the remnants of the Castro regime could no longer

---

The Global Actors of 2020

- *Nation States*

- *Hybrid States*

- *Global Corporations*

- *Global Corporate Alliances*

- *Traditional International Organizations, like the U.N.*

- *Regional Organizations that share power between nations and the Globals, like the New OAS*

- *Transnational Criminal Organizations*

- *Mercenary Units*

---

hold onto power in Cuba. For years, the country had been failing and finally the people had enough. They rose up in rebellion and installed a new pro-democracy, pro-business government. As we know, that was the story as it originally hit the netcasts. In reality that rebellion was supported by a number of Globals. They more or less engineered the coups and the political peace that resulted. Today Cuba is a sort of hybrid country. It is not exactly a traditional nation-state, nor is it a Global. It does not act with purely national motives, or with purely business motives. It is a peaceful place with the first solid economic growth in decades. It is the first nation on earth without a national army. Its security is established and maintained by a mercenary force. So, Castro and his ilk are gone. That was something that the U.S. had wanted for decades. One is tempted to say to the U.S. Government, 'Be careful what you wish for...' Next year 'Cuba' applies for membership in the U.N. That will be an interesting debate."

"So, Dr. Krause, we have a new system in place. Perhaps it is a bit more complex than before, but not really all that different. Nation states, their power somewhat reduced...".

"Mr. Meade, haven't you been listening? Don't you appreciate the enormity of the changes that have taken place? Fifteen years ago only nation-states had the legitimate right to use force. Fifteen years ago corporations operated under the laws of each nation. Fifteen years ago national governments provided welfare. Fifteen years ago only national governments engaged in diplomacy. Imagine for one minute (if your tiny little brain is capable of it) what a person from the year 2000–a person whose loyalties were to their country of birth–would think of our time. Here are some news headlines from the past month. For just a moment, put yourself in the shoes of a U.S. citizen from the year 2000, as they would look at these news items. They would be totally confused."

Meade seemed poised to interrupt, but quickly Amanda touched her WatchAssist for the holo projection. A set of news headlines from various net and paper sources appeared in front of her and on the viewers of the audience.

SeaTrain-Vosper-Blacks Completes Purchase of Haiphong Harbor. **The 25-year associated land lease grants total corporate sovereignty over 50 square kilometers. The Hanoi Government press release states that the lease payments will set its budget on firmer ground and that the infrastructure improvements promised by the Globals will bring new prosperity to the region. Further on, the Government asserts that there is substantial difference between national and corporate sovereignty and that is proved by the clause demanding the removal of mercenary forces within three months of treaty termination.**

Maxicorp Aircraft Denied Overflight Rights of France. **The French Government claims that it has nothing to do with Maxicorp activities in Algeria. A Maxicorp spokesperson said in an interview, "That is certainly not the way we see the situation. The people of Algeria have suffered under French Imperialism for decades. Now that they show a bit of independence, thanks to the economic growth they have achieved, the French resent their new Foreign Economic Status laws giving our corporation preferential trade rights."**

Kansas Legislature Officially Adopts Biblical Names For All Towns and Cities. **The Globals acquiesce, the zip codes remain unchanged. The U.S. Congress is in an uproar. "This is outrageous," said U.S. Senator Gessert (New Rep – Maine). "The cost of changing all those maps and addressing systems will be a huge burden on the rest of the population. This is taking states' rights to preposterous ends. I don't think they could afford to do this if the Globals were not underwriting their state budget."**

Bahrain Prince Closes Deal on the Purchase of 16 EuroFighter IIs. **The final destination is rumored to be an unknown mercenary unit. The Prince was quoted as saying, "This purchase will help provide for the ultimate defensive in-**

dependence of my country." Since his country does not possess the infra-structure for a modern air force, that statement left a lot of room for speculation.

Bomb Attack Mars the World Series between the Cleveland Indians and the Intel Chips. FBI sources confirm that the bomb parts were made in Southeast Asia, but say that proves nothing. The bomb went off at 2:00 a.m. in a maintenance tunnel at Jacobs Field in Cleveland. No one was injured at that time of night, but the stadium has suffered serious structural damage. No one took responsibility for the blast, but the facilities of the Indians' owners, Shell-Aramco, have been the target of terrorist attacks in South East Asia for over a decade.

The Atlantic Corporate Alliance Grants 4 Billion Euros in Aid to Needy Countries. The press release encourages other Globals to join in following the U.S. Congress cut-off of all foreign aid. "If the United States government is going to turn its back of starving children all over the world, then someone must step in and help. As a global corporate citizen, we can think of no better use of our profits than the nourishment of needy families. This donation is a stopgap measure. We call on all our fellow Globals to set up a world-wide trust fund to help the needy."

"Yes, Dr. Krause, I think I see your point. We have a new system in place. Perhaps it is a bit more complex than before, but not really all that different. Nation-states, their power somewhat reduced, work hand-in-hand with the Globals, their power very modestly enhanced, for peaceful and growing markets. Probably that growth would improve if the U.S. would rejoin...."

Amanda tuned him out. I give up. It is three minutes until the end of the show. This is the only thing he has rehearsed. It is the key message his bosses want to get out. I might as well shut up, because anything I say at this point will be "reformatted." I wish I could have told the Brazil story. Not many know it. But it would cost my career, or worse. Back in 2017, the U.S. levied some very restrictive new regulations on Coca-Cola. Coke used all the influence they had in Washington, but nothing worked. Six months later there was a huge anti-U.S. riot in Brazil after the Ambassador's car was seen in a hit and run accident that killed a vagrant. Two Marine guards were killed and dozens of Brazilians injured in the attack on the Embassy. The U.S. Ambassador was asked to leave. Diplomatic relations were suspended and Brazil engineered a vote to suspend the U.S. from the OAS. Then things quieted down. The U.S. apologized, reparations were paid, and things returned to normal. Within a week, the regulations that Coca-Cola disliked so much were rescinded. When Coke could not use the regular channels, they found another way.

With such a complex, ever-shifting pattern of political, economic, and business motives and alliances among the hundreds of globals and traditional nations, the rules really are changing, if there are any rules.

And if Colonel Schroeder is right, global events and power structures may be moving is some very ugly ways. It should be an interesting meeting. I wonder just how much I can trust the CEO-Colonel of WorldWide Spetz?

BIBLIOGRAPHY

Bass, Thomas A., *Reinventing The Future: Conversations With The World's Leading Scientists*, Addison-Wesley Publishing Company, Reading, 1994.

Becker, Jurek, *Jakob the Liar*, Penguin Group, New York, 1999.

Casti, John L., *Complexification: Explaining a Paradoxical World Through the Science of Surprise*, HarperCollins Publishers, New York, 1994.

Cooper, Arthur, *Lipo And Tu Fu*, Penguin Books Ltd., London, 1973.

Davidson, H.R. Ellis, *Myths And Symbols In Pagan Europe: Early Scandinavian And Celtic Religions*, Syracuse University Press, Syracuse, 1988.

Davis, Jacquelyn A., and Michael J. Sweeney, *Strategic Paradigms 2025: U.S. Security Planning for a New Era*, The Institute for Foreign Policy Analysis, Inc., Cambridge, 1999.

Fadiman, James and Robert Frager, *Essential Sufism*, HarperCollins Publishers, Inc., New York, 1997.

Gell-Mann, Murray, *The Quark And The Jaguar: Adventures In The Simple And The Complex*, W.H. Freeman and Company, New York, 1994.

Graham, A.C., *Poems Of The Late T'Ang*, Penguin Books Ltd., London, 1965.

Grant, Michael, *The Ancient Mediterranean*, Meridian, New York, 1969.

Hawkes, David, *The Songs of the South: An Ancient Anthology Of Poems By Qu Yuan And Others*, Penguin Books Ltd., London, 1985.

Hawking, Stephen, *A Brief History Of Time: From The Big Bang To Black Holes*, Bantam Books, New York, 1988.

Heaney, Seamus, *Beowulf*, Farrar, Straus and Giroux, New York, 1988.

Leakey, Richard, *The Origin of Humankind*, BasicBooks, New York, 1994.

Macqueen, J.G., *The Hittites and their Contemporaries in Asia Minor*, Thames and Hudson, New York, 1975.

McEvedy, Colin, *The Penguin Atlas of Ancient History*, Penguin Books, London, 1967.

Schmandt-Besserat, Denise, *How Writing Came About*, University of Texas Press: Austin, 1992.

Silver, Brian L., *The Ascent Of Science*, Oxford University Press, Oxford, 1998.

Snell, Daniel C., *Life In The Ancient Near East*, Vail-Ballou Press, Binghamton, 1997.

Stringer, Christopher and Clive Gamble, *In Search of the Neanderthals*, Thames and Hudson, New York, 1993.

Townsend, Richard F., *The Aztecs*, Thames & Hudson Inc., New York, 1993.

Walker, Brian Brown, *The Tao Te Ching of Lao Tzu*, St. Martin's Press, New York, 1995.

Whincup, Greg, *The Heart Of Chinese Poetry: China's Greatest Poems Newly Translated*, Anchor Press, New York, 1987.

Wilson, Edward O., *Consilience: The Unity Of Knowledge*, Alfred A. Knopf, New York, 1998.

ENDNOTES

[1] "A Dearth of Data at the ECB," *The Economist*, April 22, 2000, p. 74.

[2] "Snooping's Not Just For Spies Any More," *New York Times*, April 23, 2000, p. 6.

[3] *Jakob the Liar*, Jurek Becker, Penguin Books, NY, NY 1999.

[4] *The Heart of Chinese Poetry*, Greg Whincup, Anchor Press, NY 1987. p. 71.

[5] *The Jade Mountain*, Translated by Witter Bynner, Anchor Books, NY, 1964. p. 121.

[6] *The Washington Post*, May 10, 2000. Remaining copy below:

No one in Congress had proposed enacting anything like House Bill 602-P, but in reaction to the public sentiment, Rep. Fred Upton (R-Mich.) has drafted a proposal to block the idea.

This morning, as part of a larger debate about Internet taxation, the House Commerce Committee is scheduled to vote on Upton's bill, delivering a lesson in the metaphysics of democracy, New Media-style: So long as enough people with computers believe in something and also believe it is bad, someone will rise up to stop it.

"The perception really does become the reality," said Upton, noting that the e-mail barrage began more than a year ago and has remained constant. "The reality is that more people are communicating with us on this than on any other subject — more than abortion, more than Elian, more than gas prices... My legislation stops it in its tracks."

While there is no Schnell-like plan to impose a tax for using the Internet, the idea doesn't come from nowhere. It has been raised by local telephone companies, which argue that Internet service providers are unfairly bypassing the charges that long-distance phone companies must pay for using their local lines.

Upton said that when he checked with the Federal Communications Commission, he was horrified to learn that the agency does in fact have the authority to impose such "access charges."

The FCC, though, has promised it has no plan to impose Internet fees and said so again yesterday. "Congress always has the right to legislate policy, and we respect that," said Joy Howell, an FCC spokesman, "but in this case we think it's superfluous."

Given the FCC's position, some lobbyists privately accused the Republican leadership of embracing the cause of the Schnell believers as a handy straw man, a way to grandstand on a popular – if imagined — issue. Capitol Hill sources noted that the Commerce Committee is under pressure from House Majority Leader Richard K. Armey (R-Tex.) to quickly adopt several Internet-related bills. Killing a tax, even a merely potential tax, would add to the trophy case.

But Republican leaders dismissed talk that Upton's bill is a fix to a nonexistent problem. They note that some local phone companies have brought lawsuits aimed at forcing the FCC to impose access charges on Internet service providers. Moreover, the FCC has said that if the Internet continues to grow as a means of transmitting voice telephone calls, it might then consider imposing access charges, a position the Bell companies embrace.

"The Internet is a convenient way to bypass the local telephone system," said Roy M. Neel, president of the U.S. Telecom Association, which represents the Bells and other local companies. He said Upton's bill could undermine federal subsidies for rural telephone service.

A spokesman for the House Commerce chairman, Rep. Thomas J. Bliley Jr. (R-Va.), called access charges for Internet service providers "a bad idea," adding that "we want to enshrine into law that the commission shall not have the power to impose" them.

Upton's sentiments exactly. Even if the congressional advocate for the fees is a fictional character.

"I've had friends say — and my wife has asked — 'Fred, is it true?' "Upton said. "My bill soothes their fears."

[7] "Kashmir comes to Birmingham," *The Economist*, April 22, 2000.

[8] "In Latvia, World War II Isn't Quite Over," The Washington Post, March 20, 2000.

[9] The historical material for this chapter is taken from *The Aztecs*, Richard F. Townsend. Thames and Hudson Ltd, London, 2000.

[10] "Montecuhzoma" is generally agreed among scholars as the more accurate English rendition of the familiar name "Montezuma."

[11] Townsend, p. 200 quoting from *The Discovery and Conquest of Mexico*, Bernal Diaz del Castillo. Farrar, Straus, and Cudahy, NY, 1956.

[12] By "Internet" here, we mean the future network infrastructure of the world, whatever its future technical manifestation may be.

[13] *Beowulf*, Seamus Heaney; Farrar, Straus and Giroux, NY. p. 109.
[14] Ibid. p. xvi.
[15] Ibid. p. Ix.
[16] Ibid. p. xvi.